COUNTRY LIVING
cottage gardens

COUNTRY LIVING
cottage gardens

Toby Musgrave

photography by Jerry Harpur and Marcus Harpur

HEARST BOOKS
A Division of Sterling Publishing Co., Inc.
New York

To Vibeke, thank you for all your
love, laughter and patience, and
above all for being my wife.

Text copyright © Toby Musgrave 2004
Design and photographs copyright © Jacqui Small
2004

First published in 2004 by Jacqui Small an imprint
of Aurum Press

Publisher Jacqui Small
Editorial Manager Kate John
Design Maggie Town, Beverly Price
Illustration Lizzie Sanders, Ann Winterboatham,
Sally Pinhey, David Ashby
Production Geoff Barlow

The Library of Congress cataloged the hardcover
edition as follows:
Musgrave, Toby.
  Country living cottage gardens / by Toby
Musgrave.
     p. cm.
Includes index.
  ISBN 1-58816-312-1
  1. Cottage gardens. 2. Cottage gardening. I. Title:
Cottage gardens. II. Title.
  SB454.3.C67M87 2004
  635--dc22
                              2003021003

10 9 8 7 6 5 4 3 2 1

First Paperback Edition 2007
Published by Hearst Books
A Division of Sterling Publishing Co., Inc.
387 Park Avenue South, New York, NY 10016

Country Living and Hearst Books are trademarks of
Hearst Communications, Inc.

www.countryliving.com

For information about custom editions, special sales,
premium and corporate purchases, please contact
Sterling Special Sales Department at 800-805-5489
or specialsales@sterlingpub.com.

Distributed in Canada by Sterling Publishing
c/o Canadian Manda Group, 165 Dufferin Street
Toronto, Ontario, Canada M6K 3H6

Manufactured in China

Sterling ISBN 13: 978-1-58816-661-6
ISBN 10: 1-58816-661-9

Note: While the instructions in this book are
believed to be accurate and true at the time of going
to press, they cannot replace the advice of specialists
in appropriate cases. Therefore the author cannot
accept any legal responsibility or liability for any
loss, damage or injury cause by reliance on the
accuracy of such instructions.

contents

foreword

No style of garden says "welcome home" more warmly than a cottage garden. Filled with a colorful patchwork of familiar flowers, herbs, fruits, and vegetables, these multitasking spaces never set out to impress us with a flash of wealth or a show of worldly sophistication. Instead, they work their way into our hearts and imaginations through sheer spunk, pluck, and personality. And there they remain.

above Down the garden path: Every element of a cottage garden, from its entrance gateway through its layout to its planting and use, is an enticement to garden in a way that is charming, elegant, romantic, and, above all, rewarding and fun.

right Anne Hathaway's cottage near Stratford-upon-Avon was the home to William Shakespeare's wife before their marriage. Today, it encapsulates the "rural idyll" of the cottage garden, the rustic-timbered and thatched Elizabethan cottage, together with its climbing rose, set off by an ebullient display of summer flowers.

left A study in superlatives: East Lambrook Manor in Somerset was the "laboratory" of Margery Fish, who redefined cottage gardening in the 20th century. With its eye-catching birdbath and exuberant yet carefully composed planting, this is one of many compartments filled with interesting plants—such as *Sedum erythrostictum* 'Frosty Morn', *Centaurea montana* 'Carnea', and *Iris pallida* 'Argentea Variegata'— that she helped to conserve for future generations.

opposite The traditional cottage garden has a formal structure, whose edges are softened by its plantings of old-fashioned plants that imbue it with a sense of timelessness. This garden on Nantucket Island also demonstrates that large expanses of a carefully selected single genus can do the job equally effectively as Mrs. Fish's ebullient mix (left).

Today, more than ever, we look to the garden as an extension of "home" and as an escape from the stresses of our busy routines. Where else but in the garden can we find food for the body and nourishment for the soul in such proximity to our kitchens and living rooms? When we create a cottage style garden, we are following in the footsteps of generations of American gardeners who came before us: The earliest New England settlers, Prairie homesteaders, and countless poets, writers, and painters found sustenance and solace in these unpretentious little portions of Paradise. Their history traces back centuries and crosses oceans, yet these casual, one-of-a-kind spaces remain, in their practicality, individuality, and regional diversity, the ideal gardens for today's American home. They respect the land and revive the spirit.

Those of us who grow our own vegetables, fruits, and flowers today rarely do so because we would otherwise do without them: Our local markets are well supplied with produce that is shipped to us quickly and inexpensively from all over the world. And yet we still crave the food for the soul that the traditional cottage garden provides. We take comfort in knowing that, on no more than a quarter of an acre (and it can be done on much less), we can reconnect with the basic human needs to live in tune with the seasons, nurture life, and indulge the senses. Cottage gardeners can gather roses, pick berries, and pluck Brandywine tomatoes straight from the vine—it's all waiting right outside the door.

Over the past 200 years, the cottage garden has evolved from a tool of survival to a true comfort zone. We hope the garden details, plant lists, and illustrated plans that Toby Musgrave presents in this volume will encourage you to create a cottage garden of your own. They don't require a large outlay of cash to start: They are often begun from a few packets of seed or from cuttings or transplants passed along to us by friends and fellow gardeners. And they don't demand countless hours to maintain: They celebrate the art of imperfection and give us back in

harvest, fragrance, beauty, and pure enjoyment far more than they ever ask in return. They are havens from our everyday cares and an invitation to be in closer touch with the earth. They are expressions of individuality and celebrations of the seasons. The very best, in fact, are works of art.

On the following pages, Toby Musgrave has gathered a collection of gardens from Maine to Tasmania, France to Phoenix: Each one is different, each one demonstrates the simple pleasures of the cottage garden, and each one has the quality of making all who enter feel "at home." We hope that they will make you will feel welcomed—and inspired.

Nancy Mernit Soriano
Editor-in-Chief, *Country Living*

the cottage garden

Nostalgia, emotion, and romance all take root in the "traditional" cottage garden. In the midst of the hustle and bustle of our fast-paced lives, the vision of an unpretentious landscape filled with color, fragrance, birdsong, and the drowsy hum of honeybees takes on an almost mythic quality. In our mind's eye, there is an arched gateway of clipped privet or a picket fence covered in climbing roses. A straight path of brick, gravel, or grass leads to a quaint, whitewashed cottage. And the flowerbeds that flank the walkway spill forth with an effervescent mix of self-sown annuals, perennials, and herbs—all simply squeezed in wherever space permits. Vegetables, vines, outbuildings, and ornaments add to the harmonies and contrasts of form, color, and texture that make

the cottage garden a unified whole, an oasis of calm, a place to which we would dearly like to escape.

As the physical manifestation of a spiritual ethos, the cottage garden style captures the essence of what an ornamental garden should be—a place of beauty and repose, a personal haven. It enables us to get in touch with the soil, to enjoy the humble but hugely rewarding pleasures of sowing seed and taking cuttings, of nurturing plants and watching them grow, and of harvesting and eating home-grown produce. It is exactly because the style is so practical, versatile, and flexible that there can be no prescribed formula for creating such a paradise. Interpretations vary to suit personal tastes as well as local conditions. The cottage garden is as much at home in an urban setting as in a rural one, as comfortable in a big space as in a small one. For more than 200 years, the style has been evolving, drawing inspiration from its rich legacy as well as from newly discovered plants and regional materials. Whatever its guise, the cottage garden remains straightforward to create, easy to attain, and rewardingly fuss-free to care for.

There are no firm records of traditional cottage gardens prior to the second half of the 18th century. Certainly small gardens did exist in Europe well before this, but they were either made by the wealthy (often behind the protection of medieval castle walls) or by people who relied on them for food. The cottage garden, in contrast, has always been the domain of those with the desire— and sufficient leisure time and financial resources—to combine the productivity of a well-tended orchard or vegetable plot with the

far left The garland of the climbing rose and blue *Abutilon* gives this open doorway a very welcoming air. Ascending the steps to enter, visitors' legs will brush past the carefully positioned herbs, perfuming the air and creating an even more relaxing atmosphere.

left The ethos of the cottage garden is wholly applicable to today, as this garden in Connecticut amply demonstrates.. With its intriguing shelter, comfortable chairs, and lush planting, this is a place to enjoy practising the art of cultivation and also to relax and take pleasure in the fruits of one's labors.

far left A cottage garden is a melody of different notes that play harmoniously together, and attention to detail is critical. Here, the selection and arrangement of plants, the garden structure into which they slot, and the ornaments that act as counterpoints, unite in a well-balanced whole.

left The garden of Danish artist Anne Just, where the formal canal reflects the lackadaisical dahlias, demonstrates both that contemporary and traditional can be happy bedfellows; and that the cottage garden is the perfect style for juxtaposing formal and informal. And, personally, I believe no garden should be without water.

aesthetic pleasures of an ornamental flower garden. Which is not to say that these attractively planted gardens were not hard working. In North America, in fact, cottage gardens numbered among the settlers' essential tools of survival. Aided in many regions by Native Americans, who shared their knowledge of indigenous plants and cultivation techniques with the newcomers, the colonists planted utilitarian gardens that produced the fruits, vegetables, and herbs they needed to ensure their survival. Characteristically, these early gardens were situated close to the house, were enclosed by a wooden rail or pale fence to keep out roving hogs and cattle, and were filled with as many types of vegetables and flowers as there was room for.

In this pattern of planting, the colonists were following a tradition well established in Europe. If we take a few steps back in time and look at the range of plants available to the medieval garden maker, there is already evidence of small gardens that were expected to fulfill both aesthetic and utilitarian needs. Literary sources of the period, including Alexander Neckam's (1157–1217) *De Naturis Rerum* and *De Laudibus Divinae Sapientiae*, which were in circulation by 1200, list about 140 taxa in cultivation. This number had increased to more than 200 by the 16th century. The majority of these were "multi-skilling" plants, fulfilling a culinary, domestic, or medicinal role as well as an ornamental one.

By the final quarter of the 16th century, gardeners in England had already demonstrated evidence of a trait that continues to define British gardens: a deep love of flowers. With only small gardens at their disposal, English gardeners developed a particular fondness for small hardy plants, with anemone, auricula, carnation, hyacinth, pansy, polyanthus, ranunculus, dianthus (sweet William), and tulip topping their list of favorites. Such was the passion for certain flowers and the obsession with perfection that particularly fine new specimens of sought-after plants were known to change hands for up to a month's wages. There are even accounts of growers dying from hypothermia in harsh winters when scarce blankets were used to protect highly desired plants from frost rather than keep bodies warm.

English cottage gardeners and gentleman gardeners alike shared a love of flowers. And they brought their passion for plants—and many of their favorite specimens as well—with them when they immigrated to colonial America. According to G. Taylor, in *Old Fashioned Gardening* (1912), Colonial American cottage gardens were planted with a colorful array of plants familiar in European gardens, including "gillyflowers [carnations], holly hocks, sweet bryer, lavender cotton, white satten or honestie, English roses, fether few [feverfew], comferie [comfrey], celandine." These were all jumbled in with the "lettice and sorrel, Marygold, parsley, chervil, burnet, savory, time [thyme], sage, spear mint, penny royal, smalledge, fennel." Throughout the 18th and early 19th centuries, the colonies, and later the fledgling American nation, experienced rapid economic growth. Prosperity and generally peaceful conditions allowed ornamental gardens to develop further. Yet despite an increase in size and lavishness, Federal-period style remained practical in spirit to the cottage gardens that preceded them.

While the meticulously restored gardens at Thomas Jefferson's Monticello and George Washington's Mount Vernon offer fine examples of professionally designed landscapes influenced by European models, more typical gardens of the time were far more economically laid out. The attorney Benjamin Waller's circa 1807 creation in Williamsburg, Virginia, for example, clearly shows the continued influence of the cottage garden style. Situated close to the house, the neatly arranged garden is made up of a series of small, geometric, box-edged beds filled with roses and flowering bulbs, fruit trees, a grape arbor, and generous plantings of currants, berries, herbs, and vegetables. Such a garden would have been typical of the period, whether intended to serve a gentleman who was striving to develop a "lifestyle" or to meet the needs of laborers for whom providing wholesome food was of prime concern.

left Conventionally, a cottage garden was as much about edible plants as ornamental ones. Today, the balance is individual choice. What has not changed is how attractive a productive garden is. These box-edged beds would look equally striking filled with a riot of perennials and annuals.

opposite A great advantage of a closely planted display is reduced weeding. But should a self-sown ornamental pop up uninvited, so long as it brings something to the party (such as the white daisy among the lychnis), why not leave it?

In Britain, it wasn't until the late 18th century—a time when making landscape gardens was all the rage among the wealthy cognoscenti—that the cottage itself was first considered a garden feature in its own right. In 1794, two neighbors, Richard Payne Knight (1750–1824) and the more talented Sir Uvedale Price (1747–1829), published, respectively, *The Landscape* and *An Essay on the Picturesque*. Both men advocated the Picturesque approach to grounds design in which the cottage, and in particular the cottage orné (literally an ornamental cottage), was deemed a welcome addition to the landscape. But the cottage evolved as more than simply a desirable landscape feature; it became home to certain members of the gentry, particularly those with limited means who could not afford a grand house and estate. In America, the virtues of well-planned gardens for rural and suburban properties were celebrated in the writings of Andrew Jackson Downing (1815–1852), a former nurseryman from Newburgh, New York. As editor of *The Horticulturist* magazine from 1846 until his death, Downing used his bully pulpit to bring Americans to a new level of "taste." His *Treatise on the Theory and Practice of Landscape Gardening Adapted to North America* (1841) promoted a new appreciation for the type of rural cottages and picturesque suburban landscapes illustrated in house pattern books like those published by Andrew Jackson

Davis in 1837 (*Rural Residences*). Aimed at the client rather than the professional homebuilder, these house pattern books brought new attention to the landscape as an important part of the suburban home. Later works, including those by Calvert Vaux (*Villas and Cottages*, 1857) and Frank J. Scott (*The Art of Beautifying Suburban Home Grounds of Small Extent*, 1870) introduced some exotic plant choices to the mix, but the overall look owed much to the unpretentious cottage gardens of the past.

The cottage idyll has often attracted the romantic soul. Writers, poets, and painters have all celebrated the charms of the small lot made fragrant with roses, fruit trees, and vines. William Shakespeare's works are peppered with references that may have been inspired by either his father's garden or by the landscape around Anne Hathaway's cottage. William Wordsworth (1763–1835), who moved to Dove Cottage in England's rural Lake District in December 1799, lived there with his wife, Mary, and sister, Dorothy, until May 1808, during the period of his greatest poetic achievements. The whitewashed structure, strewn with climbing roses, honeysuckle, and scarlet runner beans, brought great joy to the family and was admired by many visitors, including Walter Scott, Samuel Coleridge, and the Wordsworths' successor in the cottage, Thomas De Quincey. In 1835, one of America's best-known writers, Washington Irving

(1783–1859), bought a humble 18th century cottage on the east bank of the Hudson River near Tarrytown, New York, and set out to transform it into a country estate. A Spanish-style bower and Dutch-style step gables distinguish the wisteria-draped façade, while picturesque pathways and plantings instilled the grounds with a sense of romance. For the rest of his life, Irving used the cottage, which he named Sunnyside, as his home base. Here, mere steps from the railroad tracks that carried passengers to and from New York City each day, he established a garden, entertained guests, and lived the life of a country gentleman.

As the Victorian era progressed and cities became increasingly wealthy, industrialized, and congested, gardening became a popular pastime. The country cottage that remained the home of artisans, craftsmen, and workers had been elevated to a picturesque ideal, a tranquil refuge for a group of educated and wealthy gentlefolk and artists who sought to live tasteful, thoughtful, and artistic lives of relative simplicity. Their writings provide a clear picture of the old-fashioned gardens they preferred. Hedges are shaped to harmonize with the garden, while a tree or two cast shade. The cottage itself provided support for trained fruit trees—apples, pears, cherries, plums, and apricots, and was also smothered with climbers such as honeysuckle, roses, clematis, convolvulus (morning glory), jasmine, passionflower, and ivy. Hardy plants continued to be the backbone of the ornamental display. Named perennials included hollyhocks, campanulas (bellflowers), peonies, pinks, lilies-of-the- valley, Michaelmas daisies (the native American aster), and polyanthus. Annuals included mignonette, stocks, sweet peas, and larkspur; among the bulbs were lilies, tulips, crocuses, and snowdrops.

One new introduction was bedding plants. By the 1830s scores of nursery catalogues were already offering a huge selection of tender annuals and perennials from which to choose, the bounty from plant hunters who had, from the mid-17th century, explored South America and South Africa. Among

right The geometric regularity of the herringbone pattern of the brickwork contrasts with the gently sinuous path, which entices one to move through the color-co-ordinated planting display, including *Sisynchrium strictum* 'Aunt May', *Ballota pseudodictamnus*, *Eryngium giganteum*, and *Lychnis coronaria* 'Alba', toward an ornamental rustic wood bench.

the bedding plants they brought back home with them were pelargoniums (geraniums), dahlias, salvias, zinnias, China asters, and Brompton stocks. Perhaps surprisingly, period books do not mention vegetables, though one must assume crops were planted! There would have been a wide selection of seasonal vegetables—root crops, brassicas, lettuces, legumes, and alliums, together with herbs and bush fruits such as strawberries and raspberries. In addition to flora there were fauna—a pig, poultry, often bees, and, in a larger garden, a cow.

In the grand houses and mansions (often referred to by their owners as "cottages") of wealthy Victorians, the fad for bedding plants grew apace, and among the fashion-conscious crowd, hardy, old-fashioned plants were relegated to the cutting garden or to the borders lining the paths in the kitchen garden. They were replaced in the ornamental garden by tender annuals planted to produce the most striking color effects—the brighter, even garish, and more contrasting the better. Sooner or later, however, the wheel of fashion always turns full circle, and the voices of discontent were inevitably raised against such excesses of the Gilded Age.

The movement to return to a more natural form of gardening, in which hardy, old-fashioned plants played a central role, was championed by aesthetes on both sides of the Atlantic who rued the loss of lovely old-fashioned flowers and more natural planting schemes. Cottage style plantings found a new

left The cottage garden style is often considered synonymous with hardy perennials, but one of the reasons for its long-term success is that it has always welcomed new plants into the fold, be they tender exotics such as the *Canna* and the cosmos, or dwarf conifers. Additionally, the blurred edges, as the plants flop over the path, introduce a subtle softness.

opposite Mother Nature is incomparable and never ceases to be a germane instructor, teaching valuable lessons about the aesthetics of plant arrangement. So much so that we often set out to imitate her, as here where a grass path cuts through a wildflower meadow dominated by the white and the yellow of ox-eye daisy and cat's ear.

place in the hearts of innovative gardeners, including the hugely influential designer Gertrude Jekyll (1843–1932). Miss Jekyll, remembered primarily for her innovative application of painterly color theory to planting arrangements, "painted" gardens with flowers and foliage. Largely responsible for repopularizing the herbaceous border in England, she had a wide knowledge and understanding of rural traditions and was strongly influenced by cottage gardens. "They have a simple and tender charm that one may look for in vain in gardens of greater pretension," she wrote. "And the old garden flowers seem to know that there they are seen at their best."

Miss Jekyll influenced garden makers across the world—from Edna Walling in Australia to Beatrix Farrand in the United States. Old-fashioned gardens were "rediscovered" in the United States in the 50 years between the Civil War and the First World War, when beds and borders filled with a practical mix of favorite flowers, vegetables, and herbs once more captured the romantic imagination. Influenced by an aesthetic trend similar to the Arts and Crafts Movement in Britain, these poetic, practical plots had their antecedents in the American cottage garden of the 17th and 18th centuries. The writer Anne Dudley Warner (*Gardening by Myself*, 1872), the poet Celia Thaxter (*An Island Garden*, 1894) and a whole generation of American Impressionist painters numbered among the voices extolling the simple pleasures of making things grow and the importance of domestic refinement over worldly riches or industrial superiority. In suburbs and artists' colonies from Connecticut to California, old-fashioned gardens served as outdoor parlors and salons, with the floral paths and arbors of the cottage garden furnishing the "decoration."

One of the most influential of all gardens made in the 20th century is Sissinghurst in Kent, England. The perfect union of Harold Nicolson's classical mind and Vita Sackville-West's romantic bent, and its "rooms" have much to inspire the cottage garden maker. It remains, however, a large garden of small

compartments. The most pioneering cottage gardener of the century was Margery Fish (1892–1969), who devised a whole new form in her garden at East Lambrook Manor, Somerset, which she evolved from 1938 until her death. With its nooks and crannies offering a range of microclimates, the garden that Mrs. Fish created realized her ambition to surround her home with a manageable garden filled with interesting plants that looked attractive all year round. Mrs. Fish recounted her experience of "weekend cottage gardening" in *We Made a Garden* (1956), an influential book that remains recommended reading for all cottage gardeners.

The history of the cottage garden continues to inspire and instruct. But, now as always, the form these infinitely adaptable gardens take depends entirely on the vision of the gardener. It is a style that says as much about the person who creates the garden as it does about any of the plants, ornaments, or architectural features the site captures. Utility, versatility, and lasting charm all await in the cottage gardens of the future.

designing by
theme

traditional

The words "cottage garden" bring to mind a mixture of ornamental and edible plants, grown in a relatively small space. Traditional design balances beauty and practicality in a floral and vegetable bonanza, into which today's cottage gardener can integrate space to escape and recharge, to relax and revivify.

opposite A truly international style: This "traditional" cottage garden is in South Africa. It works because it takes fullest advantage of the cottage garden values of flexibility, individuality, and pragmatism. Filled with plants that succeed in this climate, such as hibiscus, it retains a cottage feel while exuding an air of exoticism.

In this design (the plan is shown on pages 28–29) the garden layout is informally formal, with a traditional quatrefoil arrangement of beds centered around the circular pool. This has echoes of a well or a dipping pool (a reservoir of water from which gardeners filled their watering cans before the advent of the garden hose), but, with its Mercury fountain, it is now an object of ornament. At the far end of the garden is a wooden pergola smothered in sweet smelling climbers, but in place of a bench or any other seat, because of the juxtaposition of the utility areas—one containing cold frames and compost bins; the other, a greenhouse—it features instead a statue of Flora overseeing this horticultural bounty. This classical figure provides a link with the Mercury fountain and serves as a terminal focal point, which could be illuminated at night for even greater impact. The bird topiaries introduce a traditional touch, as do the standard-trained roses, while the willow tepee plantframes bring the rustic feel up to date. Other appropriate focal points would be a birdbath, sundial or armillary sphere, or a dovecote.

Broken flagstones or flat stones gathered from fields would have made inexpensive paths in the traditional cottage garden. The most authentic paving surface in England is Yorkstone, laid in a "crazy" pattern, that is to say broken (but large) pieces of flag arranged randomly. The gaps between the stones can be grouted with cement or planted with herbs such as thyme (*Thymus vulgaris*) or chamomile (*Chamaemelum nobile*), which scent the air when walked on. An alternative traditional path material, although more messy in a wet climate, is beaten earth. More practical choices are regularly cut stone flags, brick, or reconstituted stone slabs. I do not recommend gravel

or crushed stone, as they migrate and become clogged with earth if walked over in grubby boots. They are also difficult to push a wheelbarrow through.

Flanking the paths, the 12 in (30 cm) high hedge of the evergreen French lavender (*Lavandula stoechas*) imparts year-round structure, and in summer the flowers will introduce form, color, and scent, as well as attracting bees. Alternative hedging plants include English lavender in blue or white (*L. angustifolia* and *L.a.* 'Alba'), dwarf box (*Buxus sempervirens* 'Suffruticosa') or lavender cotton (*Santolina chamaecyparissus*). Behind the hedge, contrasting with its formality and introducing another height level, is a narrow ribbon border planted with an informal, riotous mix of hardy annuals and annual herbs. These will self-sow, creating a wholly natural arrangement that can be supplemented with new favourites.

This border encapsulates the fundamental rule when planting a traditional cottage garden: the only rule is that there are no rules. It is all a matter of personal choice guided by good design principles and prevailing conditions of soil, aspect, and climate. I have chosen some of my favorite plants for this garden, and over time, I would add new favorites, experiment (especially with the vegetables), and remove those that did not thrive and so the planting would evolve as I do.

There should be no prescribed formula to the structure of a cottage garden, either. Both stone and wood are used extensively here because I like their natural and rustic feel, and as the garden matures, so they mellow, maintaining the harmonious ambience and developing a sense of timelessness. But if you like something else, and it fits with the overall garden style you are aiming for, do it! Here, a break with tradition is

below Combine variety and beauty in a rich display of colour and form. Clumps—here including *Coreopsis verticillata* 'Moonbeam', *Pennisetum*, *Tithonia rotundifolia* and *Verbena bonariensis*—give a more bold result than spot-planting.

opposite For a seasoned timelessness and stability the traditional style should make full use of natural and organic materials, which complement the old-fashioned planting, as here where the red-orange of the brick unites with the *Kniphofia*.

the enclosure of the four quarters with diamond-pattern wooden trelliswork, introduced to increase the vertical space and to help define the four different areas. The panels running the length of the garden are smothered with mixed sweet peas (*Lathyrus odoratus*) to give a mix of colors and sweet scent; however, other climbers, such as roses, clematis, jasmine (*Jasminum officinale*), honeysuckle (*Lonicera* spp.), everlasting pea (*Lathyrus sylvestris*) or passionflower (*Passiflora* spp.), could be used individually or mixed together. Aim for a screen that can be seen through, rather than a thick mat of vegetation.

The range of options for filling the four beds is almost endless: whole beds put to grass and used as an area to entertain in or as a play area; a series of planted knot gardens; beds dedicated to cut flowers for the house or to growing a favorite plant species (for example, lilies, irises, or tulips). Alternatively, the whole garden can be given over to vegetable production under the four-year rotation system: each bed is planted with a crop group—solanaceous, root, and tuberous plants; legumes and pods; alliums; and brassicas—and at the end of each season, the crops are moved one bed to the left. In the the fifth season you return to the original planting.

This plan is a compromise, with half edible crops and half ornamental plants. The diversity of vegetables and fruit is as wide as possible, both in terms of the types grown and of the length of cropping season, without making the quantities of produce so small that their cultivation would not be worth the effort. To maximize fruit yields while occupying minimal space, and to provide an ornamental display, fruit trees are trained against the warmest walls and trellis in a range of shapes, including cordons, espaliers, and fans.

At the heart of the ornamental quarters are grassy retreats—sheltered havens from the outside world; one is equipped with a garden swing, the other with a wooden table and chairs. (Additional seating is provided by the two benches hidden under wisteria-clad pergolas at either end of the cross paths.) The enclosing planting is dominated by clusters of perennials and annuals, arranged to create a jeweled display of harmonious color. A stippled and more traditional effect would be achieved by spot-planting a larger assortment of varieties.

left This garden seat entices one in to sit, rest, and enjoy the show. Its solid construction imparts a sense of immutability, creating the perfect foil to the transient seasonality of the mixed planting of herbs, annuals, and perennials, including chives (*Allium schoenoprasum*), *Digitalis purpurea* Excelsior Group, wood forget-me-not (*Myosotis sylvatica*), and *Hosta fortunei* 'Albomarginata'..

opposite top This Cambridgeshire garden perfectly encapsulates the beauty of the traditional cottage-garden planting style, which comes from its great diversity—among the plants are *Eremurus*, *Crambe cordifolia*, *Iris orientalis*, and *Dictamnus albus* var. *purpureus*—and its haphazard evolution. New additions are simply crammed in where space permits.

below A cottage garden is all about individuality. In this French garden the eye-catching metal stork introduces a contemporary and personal touch that contrasts with the traditional formality of the regular box-edged beds and their softening, effervescently pink flowering display, which is dominated by roses and delphiniums.

Plants for a traditional garden

1 *Lavandula stoechas*   **2** *Passiflora caerulea*
3 Red lettuce   **4** Green lettuce
5 Carrots   **6** Radish
7 Spring onions   **8** Brussels sprouts
9 Winter cabbage   **10** *Wisteria sinensis*
11 *Wisteria sinensis* 'Alba'   **12** *Taxus baccata*
13 *Rosa* 'Zéphirine Drouhin'
14 *Clematis* Arctic Queen ('Evitwo')
15 *Rosa gallica* 'Versicolor'
16 *Lathyrus odoratus*
17 Fan-trained pear
18 Espalier-trained apple
19 Fan-trained peach
20 Espalier-trained fig
21 Fan-trained plum
22 Double cordon-trained apples
23 Fan-trained medlar
24 Multiple cordon-trained grapevine
25 Fan-trained acid cherry
26 Tomato   **27** French beans
28 Pea   **29** Runner beans (red flowering)
30 New potatoes

Planting scheme A
Jasminum officinale
Lonicera periclymenum 'Graham Thomas'
Rosa 'Blush Rambler'

Planting scheme B
Allium schoenoprasum
Antirrhinum (mixed)
Centaurea cyanus (blue, pink & white)
Consolida ajacis (dwarf form)
Dianthus 'Musgrave's Pink'
Dianthus barbatus
Foeniculum vulgare
Lychnis flos-jovis
Mentha spicata
Myosotis sylvatica
Nigella damascena
Ocimum basilicum
Papaver commutatum
Petroselinum crispum
Salvia officinalis
Scabiosa atropurpurea
Tagetes erecta

Planting scheme C
Achillea 'Lachsschönheit' (Salmon Beauty)
Allium cristophii
Alcea rosea (pale yellow, peachy pink)
Alstroemeria (mixed)
Antirrhinum (mixed)
Campanula latifolia (white)
Cerinthe major 'Purpurascens'

Cosmos sulphureus 'Polidor'
Cynara cardunculus
Delphinium 'Fenella'
Dianthus caryophyllus
Digitalis purpurea f. *albiflora*
Dipsacus sativus
Echinacea purpurea
Eremurus spectabilis
Eremurus x isabellinus Shelford hybrids
   (white, yellow)
Freesia Super Giant Series, mixed
Geranium 'Johnson's Blue'
Helianthus annuus 'Eversun'
Isoplexis canariensis
Lilium 'Star Gazer'
Lilium regale
Lupinus 'My Castle'
Lupinus mutabilis subsp. *cruckshanksii* 'Sunrise'
Monarda 'Croftway Pink'
Phlox paniculata 'Harlequin'
Verbena bonariensis

Planting scheme D
Nymphaea 'Gonnère'
Nymphaea 'Odorata Sulphurea Grandiflora'

Planting scheme E
Agapanthus 'Lilliput'
Anthemis tinctoria 'E. C. Buxton'
Cosmos bipinnatus (pink)
Delphinium 'Sungleam'
Dianthus 'Alice'
Digitalis purpurea f. *albiflora*
Dorotheanthus bellidiformis
Echinacea purpurea
Geranium 'Johnson's Blue'
Geranium procurrens
Geranium psilostemon
Hemerocallis 'Mauna Loa'
Hemerocallis fulva 'Flore Pleno'
Limnanthes douglasii
Lychnis chalcedonica
Matthiola incana Brompton Group (mixed)
Matthiola incana East Lothian Group (mixed)
Mirabilis jalapa (white, pink, red)
Nasturtium (mixed)
Nepeta sibirica 'Souvenir d'André Chaudron'
Nicotiana alata
Nigella damascena (white)
Nigella damascena 'Miss Jekyll'
Penstemon 'Stapleford Gem'
Reseda odorata
Salvia splendens 'Rambo'
Scabiosa atropurpurea

tapestry

Informal and arbitrary, lively and vivacious, a tapestry planting effect uses small clumps, rather than painterly drifts, of old-fashioned ornamentals. Viewed en masse, the result is a wonderfully rich tapestry of color, form, and height, which relies as much on contrast as it does on harmony.

below Tapestry style on a large scale is captured perfectly. Individual specimens would be appropriate to a smaller space. Here distinct clumps of plants, from the tallest *Dahlia* to the lowest *Heuchera*, are arranged in a rich embroidery of forms.

opposite The rich red and yellow of the *Hemerocallis* complement one another, while their hot flower colors contrast with the metallic blue of *Eryngium* and leaden bloom of the poppy seed heads.

Raised beds are practical, attractive, and easy to construct, and they can make the most of a small space, giving a garden instant structure. Moreover, they retain the soil within a confined space, making maintenance easier. The material from which raised beds are constructed helps to define and anchor the garden's ambience. In a cottage garden, the most appropriate materials are natural ones—wood, woven willow (living or dead), stone, or weathered brick. For a more contemporary feel, try stainless steel, dyed concrete, colored plastic, or opaque sand-blasted glass.

A straightforward approach, and one that would give the garden a medieval feel, is serried rows of rectangular beds. This arrangement is very practical if part of the garden is to be planted with vegetables—it allows easy crop rotation and uncomplicated cultivation; and, with planning, you can calculate the quantities of produce, to maximize the range of crops while minimizing waste.

However, there are many different sources that provide inspiration for a more ornamental, tapestry garden layout—Flemish wall hangings, Elizabethan embroidery, French Renaissance wallpaper, Native American beadwork, the patterns of William Morris, or traditional American quilts—even the works of modern painters such as Ben Nicholson or Piet Mondrian. In the plan on pages 36–37, the inspiration came from a vacation in Éire, where I was captivated by the natural landscape of a patchwork of various shades of green, broken up by moss-clad stone walls, and where I saw the *Book of Kells* and ancient Celtic crosses. The former inspired the planting approach, and the latter the color schemes and the garden layout. Rather than fill the garden with a complex geometric configuration of raised beds, the intention is a wooden framework that is visually interesting when viewed both from inside the garden and from above, but which does not overwhelm. At the start and end are raised beds based on a pattern adapted from a Celtic embroidery, while the middle focal point is tiered. It is crowned with my interpretation of the Blarney Stone, a boulder from which bubbles water.

Moving water is an essential addition to any garden space, introducing dynamism, catching the light, and making a calming sound. Water also links the formal garden entrance and the informal lawn and path, in the form of a rill connecting two sunken circular basins. In the center of each of these is a small fountain.

left Bold and bright, colorful and contrasting, a tapestry planting effect is one that works as well in an informal setting as in a formal framework. It also lends itself to experimentation—for example, a display chiefly restricted to a subtle blend from one part of the color spectrum, which here includes *Iris, Allium hollandicum* 'Purple Sensation', *Phlomis russeliana, Euphorbia characias* subsp. *wulfenii,* and *Papaver atlanticum* 'Flore Pleno'.

tapestry • **33**

Another linking and unifying device is the color green. In front of the garden entrance, the framework of water-washed cobbles is filled with a patchwork of thymes, their various verdant shades reminiscent of the Irish landscape. Set within a greensward, through which meanders a curvaceous path leading to the seating area, the low close-clipped hedges of box and hyssop soften the raised beds in the center.

Again, I emphasize that the planting in a cottage garden, whatever its theme, is a very personal matter, and that you should be bound only by the rules of good design. Here, the planting is predominantly of herbaceous and bulbous species, which combine to form a soft tapestry of form and height, while their flower color captures the deep richness and diversity of medieval manuscripts, such as those in the wonderful *Book of Kells*. The plant associations are color-grouped, with a strong emphasis on tints and tones. In keeping with both the tapestry concept of individual threads and the ethos of spot planting so ingrained in cottage gardening, and to provide a heightened contrast with the blocks of color, those beds that have a mixture of plants are filled with randomly planted individual specimens.

A sense of repetition and harmony, both of which are essential for a unified garden, are introduced by the beds at the start and end of the garden. The composition of rich blues, mauves, purples, and occasional highlight "flashes" (including peonies, digitalis, astrantias, campanulas, and *Eremurus*) contrast with the white eegal lily (*Lilium regale*), placed by the door because of its wonderful scent, and the *Cardiocrinum giganteum*, which adds height to the end of the garden. Here, the "hot" hemerocallis bed draws the eye and heightens the contrast with the whites and the blocks of blue *Agapanthus* 'Bressingham Blue', which together create a rich setting for the seating. To increase height further, the beds are tiered one on top of another, and if the gardener has mobility problems, tall raised beds can be built to wheelchair height. The continuity of the perimeter border also helps unite the garden space, and with its curvaceous outline, it guides the eye along its length, thus deregulating the plot's regular shape and softening the overall geometry of the raised beds. In the

central raised beds in this plan, informal patches of five low-growing geranium species artistically echo the thyme bed. *Paeonia lactiflora* 'Sarah Bernhardt' remains visible above the tapestry of sweet peas are grown over canes laid horizontally at just below hedge height so that the flowers appear over the top of the hedge (scrambling roses would be an alternative). The small ellipse-shaped beds planted with *Lilium regale* serve as a focal point and a central link with the two ends of the garden.

Just as there are many sources of inspiration for a tapestry design, so there are different ways of approaching the tapestry planting. For example, "threads" of plants in rows can be woven together; the color range within each of the beds can be increased or changed; and a carpet of different groundcover plants can create a patchwork-quilt effect. To reduce maintenance and to increase the length of seasonal show, you could replace the predominantly perennial plantings with a mixture of architectural, flowering, and foliage shrubs, with an understory of perennials and bulbs.

Plants for a tapestry garden

1 *Agapanthus* 'Bressingham Blue'
2 *Cardiocrinum giganteum*
3 *Lonicera* x *italica*
4 *Buxus sempervirens* 'Suffruticosa'
5 *Lilium regale*
6 *Chamaemelum nobile*

Planting scheme A

Agapanthus inapertus subsp.
   intermedius
Artemisia lactiflora
Astrantia major
Astrantia major 'Sunningdale
   Variegated'
Campanula latiloba
Campanula persifolia var. *alba*
Digitalis purpurea
Digitalis purpurea f. *albiflora*
Echinacea purpurea
Eremurus x *isabellinus* Shelford
   hybrids (white & yellow)
Knautia macedonica
Miscanthus sinensis 'Gracillimus'
Paeonia officinalis 'Rubra Plena'
Paeonia suffruticosa 'Godaishu'
Verbena bonariensis

Planting scheme B

Alstroemeria (mixed)
Cosmos (pink, white and lemon-yellow)
Cynara cardunculus
Delphinium Belladonna Group
   'Cliveden Beauty'
Digitalis purpurea
Digitalis purpurea f. *albiflora*
Eremurus robustus
Eremurus x *isabellinus* Shelford
   hybrids (yellow)
Liatris spicata
Liatris spicata 'Alba'
Lilium 'Destiny'
Lilium Golden Splendor Group
Lilium regale
Lupinus Band of Nobles Series
Lychnis coronaria 'Alba'
Nicotiana alata
Verbena bonariensis
Veronica spicata 'Romiley Purple'

Planting scheme C

Geranium cinereum
Geranium dalmaticum
Geranium farreri
Geranium pylzowianum
Geranium sanguineum var. *striatum*

Planting scheme D

Hyssopus officinalis
Lathyrus odoratus (mixed)
Paeonia lactiflora 'Sarah Bernhardt'

Planting scheme E

Thymus 'Porlock'
Thymus caespititius
Thymus carnosus
Thymus herba-barona
Thymus pseudolanuginosus
Thymus serpyllum 'Annie Hall'
Thymus vulgaris

Planting scheme F

Hemerocallis 'Golden Chimes'
Hemerocallis 'Luxury Lace'
Hemerocallis 'Mauna Loa'
Hemerocallis 'Millie Schlumpf'
Hemerocallis 'Scarlet Orbit'
Hemerocallis 'Siloam Virginia Henson'
Hemerocallis 'Blushing Belle'
Hemerocallis citrina
Hemerocallis fulva 'Flore Pleno'

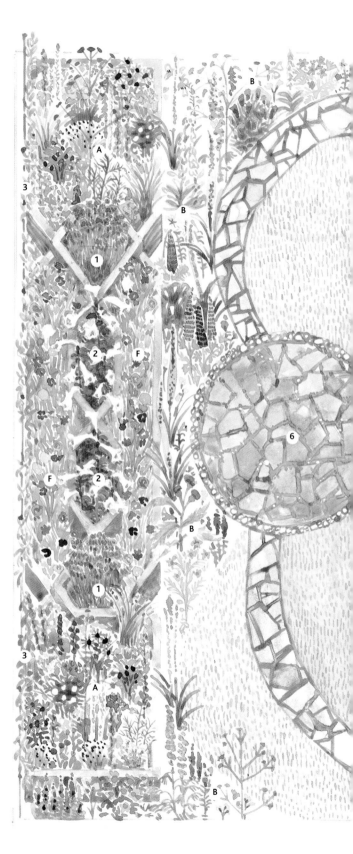

potager

Literally translated from the French, potager means "kitchen garden". But the modern potager has come to mean so much more; it is a deliberate celebration of vegetables, herbs, and fruit, grown and arranged as much for their intrinsic beauty and ornamental value as for their edibility.

above The plain palisade enclosing this French potager, together with its flower-pot ornaments and rusty iron pergola, combine with the mixture of vegetables, herbs, and ornamental plants to generate a feeling of charming rustic chic.

Until recently, edible crops were seen as the poor cousin of ornamental gardening—the realm of the vegetable geek. Now, however, influenced by concerns over pesticide residues in food and the unknown impact of genetically modified varieties, consumers have become more "product aware"; and this in turn has stimulated a huge boom in organically grown crops. For those with the space to do so, home-growing has enjoyed a revival. In many ways, the traditional cottage garden was already

on the road to being a potager in the modern sense, for productive and ornamental crops were grown together in such a way that the result was both visually attractive and utilitarian. This integration of edible and ornamental is an effect that looks especially attractive, whether the compartments are segregated as in the traditional design (see pages 28–29), or whether the boundaries are completely removed. Indeed, the latter approach, where ornamental borders and beds are enhanced with patches

right Creating a successful potager is as much about its form as its planting. In this Australian potager, the foliage of the onions, artichokes, and peppers complements the garden's straight-line geometry, which itself is enhanced by the use of different materials and the unexpected and very effective application of a change in level.

of vegetables, is very adaptable and applicable to the cottage garden style. Carrots grow next to campanulas, tomatoes are side by side with *Thalictrum*, lettuces mill around with *Linaria*, and beans grow up tepees, giving a display added height: Once again, there is no rulebook to follow. Simply find or make a space and grow what you like to eat. Note that all herbs will look great wherever you use them (although a spot in direct sunlight is preferable).

The design on pages 44–45 takes "growing to eat" a stage further and, inspired by such famous potagers as the one at Villandry in the Loire Valley, the Potager du Roi at Versailles, in France, and Rosemary Verey's garden at Barnsley House, in England, the formal layout is arranged to accommodate a broad spectrum of edible plants in a relatively small space, and in a way that makes them the star of the show. It is their individual color, form, and texture, along with the associations in which they are grouped, that provide the visual spectacle; yet with the exception of *Lavandula stoechas* (and even its flowers can be used to flavor jellies) every plant in the garden produces something to eat.

In addition to productivity, today's cottage garden—like yesterday's—should provide the gardener with space to unwind, and enjoy the fruits of their labors. Attached to the house is a raised wooden veranda, on which seats or a swing can be positioned, and at the center of this vegetative bonanza is a partially screened area accommodating a dining table and chairs and covered with a sail-like awning to provide shade and shelter from the sun or rain when dining alfresco. No space is wasted: the enclosing trellis provides support for espalier-trained apples, although any fruit trees, such a pear, plum, apricot, or peach, trained in other ways (such as a cordon, double cordon, or fan), would work equally well. The lavender foliage contrasts with the green apple leaves but is included primarily for the scent and shape of its flowers. Alternatively, the beds could become an herb garden, packed with your favorite flavorings, which scent the air on a summer evening. And to complete the relaxing ambience, there is the sound of moving water, both from the four rills within the enclosure and those terminating the cross walks. Water is also a feature when looking back at the house from the table. A series of lion-head fountains mounted in the retaining wall supporting the veranda pour into a rill that runs at the foot of the wall and beneath the wooden steps that descend into the garden.

The stone paving on which the table and chairs sit defines the area and contrasts with the herringbone brick pattern of the paths, and the bed edging. For the latter, bricks are inserted into the ground on their shortest side at an angle of 45 degrees to give a sawtooth appearance. An edging is not essential, but does clearly define the beds and keeps the soil off the paths. If available, reclaimed, weathered bricks will impart an instant maturity. Bricks can be laid in a basketweave, a 90-degree herringbone, or a horizontal bond; and pavers can be substituted for the brick for a wider range yet of patterns and colors.

A potager will be a very attractive sight even if everyday vegetables are grown; but in this case, in order to maximize the visual impact, I've chosen ornamental vegetable varieties, including purple-brown tomatoes, scarlet eggplants, yellow climbing French bean, mottled red-and-white dwarf snap bean, and pale purple asparagus. Another way to up the ante is to grow unusual vegetables that are also good lookers. Here I've used lablab beans and okra. Other possibilities are gourds, wonderberries (*Solanum* x *burbankii*), peanut (*Arachis hypogaea*), kohlrabi (*Brassica oleracea* Gongylodes Group), and salsify (*Tragopogon porrifolius*).

The planting shape within the beds is fundamental to the overall look, and different effects can be achieved by planting whole beds with an individual crop, growing in

left The ingenious curvaceous ogee dome atop the summerhouse, which picks up on the orange of the marigold flowers, provides a foil to the attractive, serried ranks of sweet corn and leeks in this Danish potager.

right As tasty as they are showy—the four types of lettuce complement the calm colours of the kohl rabi. The ever-increasing range of ornamental vegetable varieties is a bounty that gives great scope for the creation of exciting, exotic, and decorative displays.

below Relying on the careful selection of a range of tall plants, dominated in the foreground by the green bean, the simple garden form of a series of rectangular, edged beds is transformed into a rich, colorful, and beautiful show by the mixture of edibles and ornamentals.

below left Beauty is in the eye of the beholder. Gazing over a potager can make one gasp with admiration for the designer's skill; but, for my money, studying nature's ingenuity and loveliness close up, such as this squash, is just as rewarding.

left Chives are more usually grown for their edible leaves than their blooms, but they make a perfect addition to this potager, where their spherical, pinky-purple flower heads act as a perfect foil to the formally clipped box hedging and the droopy juvenile sweet corn.

below right Form and flowers in accord: The golden-green of these ripening pears harmonizes perfectly with the greenish-white of the developing *Sedum* flower heads, as does the vertical form of the wall-trained fruit trees and the horizontal woven branches of the bed edging.

opposite This Tasmanian potager is an object lesson in studying the *genius loci*, and exercising self-control. The design, with its bean poles and cordon-trained apple, is sufficiently simple and the choice of materials sympathetic, so that it is both beautiful in its own right and in perfect balance with its setting.

rows or informal drifts, or simply by mixing seed, broadcasting it, and awaiting the result! Likewise, increased numbers of fruit bushes and trees can be trained against the walls or grown in beds and underplanted with crops.

In order to maximize the visual appeal, the planting season shown is for late spring and summer cropping, but a carefully planned potager will be productive all year round (although in this case there will inevitably be parts that are either bare or semi-mature at certain times). Other seasonal ornamental vegetables include purple potatoes, purple brussels sprouts, red onions, purple and ornamental kales (which are edible), and romaine, a sculptural relative of the cauliflower.

Finally, if you have established a potager and decide that you miss flowers, it is very easy to change the display to a mixed or purely ornamental one.

Plants for a potager garden

1 Climbing French bean
(*Phaseolus vulgaris* 'Goldfield')
2 Dwarf French bean (*Phaseolus vulgaris* 'Purple Teepee')
3 Dwarf French bean (*Phaseolus vulgaris* 'Borlotto Lingua di Fuoco Nano')
4 Purple Basil (*Ocimum basilicum* var. *purpurascens*)
5 Rocket (*Eruca vesicaria* subsp. *sativa*)
6 Courgette (*Cucurbita pepo* 'Gold Rush')
7 Lettuce (*Lactuca sativa* 'Revolution')
8 Lettuce (*Lactuca sativa* 'Fristina')
9 Carrot (*Daucus carota* 'Parmex')
10 Asparagus (*Asparagus officinalis* 'Purple Jumbo')
11 Cardoon (*Cynara cardunculus*)
12 Apple (*Malus domestica* 'Red Falstaff')
13 French lavender (*Lavandula stoechas*)
14 Beet Swiss chard (*Beta vulgaris* (Cicla Group) 'Bright Lights')
15 Greek Basil (*Ocimum basilicum* var. *minimum* 'Greek')
16 Lablab bean (*Lablab purpureus* 'Ruby Moon')
17 Okra (*Abelmoschus esculentus*)
18 Tomato (*Lycopersicon esculentum* 'Black Russian')
19 Parsley (*Petroselinum crispum*)
20 Fig (*Ficus carica* 'Negro Largo')

Planting scheme A
Dill (*Anethum graveolens*)
Coriander (*Coriandrum sativum*)
Chives (*Allium schoenoprasum*)
Cumin (*Cuminum cyminum*)

Planting scheme B
Mixed sweet peppers
(*Capsicum annuum*
Grossum Group)
    'Tasty Grill Red',
    'Gypsy' (orange)
    'Tasty Grill Yellow'
    'Sweet Chocolate' (purple)

Planting scheme C
Mixed aubergines
(*Solanum melongena*)
    'Red Egg'
    'Bonica'
    'Mohican'

top Strings of drying onions hung from a post make practical albeit temporary garden ornaments.

above It's all about creating and maintaining the equilibrium between foliage, form, and flowers. Here the broad, spiky, variegated foliage of *Silybum marianum* contrasts with the thin, whip-like leaves and spherical flowers of chives.

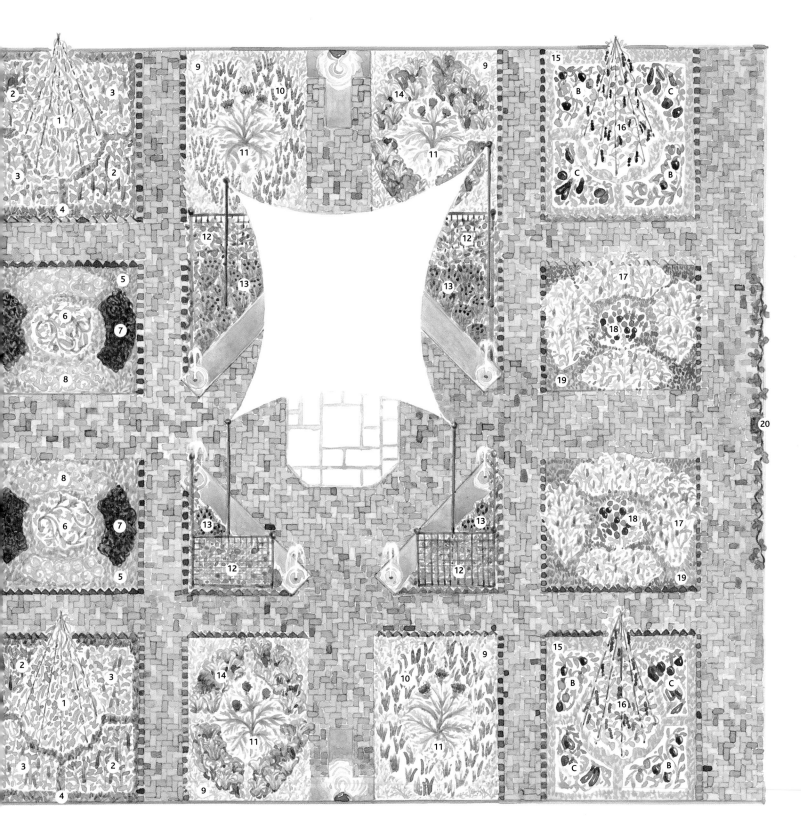

left An obelisk, perhaps a reminder of Cleopatra's love for Antony, is the eye-catcher in this romantic enclosure, where the pure white and dusky rose red of the peonies is about to be joined by the blue of the lavender, which also perfumes the air as lovers brush past its aromatic foliage.

romantic

Gardens and plants have always been associated with romance and seduction. It was in the Garden of Eden that Eve tempted Adam. In *Hamlet* we find the words "There's rosemary, that's for remembrance; pray, love, remember," while the rose has a symbolic role in *Romeo and Juliet*.

The romantic garden is a gentle garden, full of softly curved beds and borders, intersected by winding paths and filled with drifts of sweetly scented, colorful, and shapely plants. This is a place in which to be romanced by that special person when the mood takes you, yet it does not force romance down your throat. You can escape to this garden to read a book of poetry and find peace and tranquillity alone. It also has ample space in which to entertain and enjoy good company, good food, and good wine in a jovial (or perhaps bacchanalian!) atmosphere.

For all its multiple uses, the overriding theme of the layout and planting of this garden is the union of love and romance. The dominant feature is the two circular lawns with their granite sett edging, two joined "wedding bands" symbolizing the eternal cycle of love. Another symbol of love and peace is the thatched dovecote in the center of the lawns, home to a small flock of white doves. The love motif is underscored by the entwined hearts in the paving of granite setts, a unity that follows the thread in the path leading to the romantic hideaway at the far end of the garden, where the heart theme is repeated as a mosaic in the floor in front of the jasmine-smothered bower. To increase seclusion the bower is hidden within a hedged enclosure, but there are many other forms of garden structure (such as a wooden, stone, or brick summerhouse, a living willow arbor, a wrought iron ogee bower or a Crusader-style tent) that can be equipped to create the right atmosphere. If you have the space and the appropriate support, a garden swing or a hammock can be a great place to sit together.

To help create an enchanting atmosphere. where Aphrodite would feel welcome, the white marble statues provide reminders of past classical elegance, and the

calming sounds of splashing water come from the glass boulder fountain, visible through a window in the hideaway. As darkness falls, so the glass rock glows as it is illuminated from below. When the fire dishes to either side of the archways in the hedge are lit and the rest of the garden becomes invisible, with only the scent of the flowers remaining, it becomes even more intimate.

To increase the sense of romance, garden ornaments that have a special significance to you both—a sculptural piece of wood collected when walking on the beach together, an urn purchased while on vacation, a bench

above Using careful color co-ordination is a very subtle way to set a mood. Opening off the rose-strewn pergola, the wooden gateway entices visitors into this white garden, filled with *Campanula*, *Lychnis*, and foxglove, which is at once cool, calming, and dreamy— the perfect spot for seduction.

given on an anniversary—can be positioned in an eye-catching spot and illuminated at night. Introduce softer lighting with a myriad candles, oil flares, or hurricane lamps along the path, carefully positioned within the flower bed, or hung from the trees. And for the super-romantic, how about an outdoor sound system to waft passionate tunes into your beloved's ear?

The plants are grouped together in drifts to further soften the garden's appearance, and the color theme flows around the garden. Near the seating areas—by the house and in the bower—there is an emphasis on scented plants, such as dianthus, mignonette (*Reseda odorata* 'Grandiflora'), *Nicotiana alata* and jasmine (*Jasminum officinale*), and in front of the bower, a collection of roses—the most evocative of all love tokens.

Down the years, plants have been imbued with symbolic and religious meanings. For example, in Islamic gardens the plane tree (*Platanus orientalis*) was seen as the tree of life. This idea of "saying it with plants" became a great fashion in the late 18th and early 19th centuries, when it was considered the height of chivalrous, romantic, and noble behavior for a man to declare his intentions by wearing particular flowers, and for his demure beloved to respond in kind. Indeed a whole language developed by which couples could communicate their feelings without words. Today, plants continue to have meanings, most of them to do with love , so this garden is planted only with those species that have a romantic implication. The choice of "love plants" is considerably extended if tender plants are included. In colder climes these may be grown as annuals outside or, in the case of larger plants such as the gardenias, grown in containers and taken out in the summer months.

At another level, the plants that grace a romantic garden should help to create a gentle and loving mood. Plants with scented foliage or flowers are, therefore, a boon, especially those such as mignonette that are evening scented. Flowers in tints and tones are also useful —soft colors are soothing, but strong ones can be used for contrast. The same softness applies to plant form —rounded or upright forms are more appropriate than spiky architectural specimens, and with a purely personal prejudice, I would avoid gloomy conifers.

opposite top Through the gate and up the garden path to a comfortable bench where we . . . did what ever came naturally! A romantic garden is all about ambience and instilling a feeling of ease; simple is often best.

opposite centre This pretty seat for one, crowned by a climbing rose and surrounded by complementary planting including *Clematis*, *Aquilegia*, and *Phormium*, which complements the wall color, is a scented haven for one: a place to compose a love letter, plan a special event, or revel in secret memories.

opposite bottom This verdant retreat in a French monastery might be used by monks for solitary spiritual contemplation, but a similar hideaway in a romantic garden offers scope for all sorts of pleasures away from prying eyes, while the window could be aligned on a special feature or plant, fountain or statue.

left This shady sanctuary is full of congruent natural form and clipped regularity. Enlivened by the gentle sound of trickling water, the planting cunningly overcomes the problem of being overseen by close neighbors by creating a "ceiling" of greenery.

Plants for a romantic garden

1 *Gypsophila paniculata* 'Bristol Fairy'
   Gentleness, everlasting love

2 *Gardenia augusta*   A secret love

3 *Salvia splendens* (Cleopatra Series)
   'Cleopatra Blue'   I think of you

4 *Gladiolus* 'Peace'   Strong character

5 *Myosotis sylvatica*   Forget-me-not

6 *Prunus* x *subhirtella* 'Autumnalis'
   Spiritual beauty

7 *Heliotropium arborescens*
   Devotion; faithfulness

8 *Consolida ajacis* Imperial Series   Fickleness

9 *Myrtus communis*   Love

10 *Jasminum officinale*   Amiability

11 *Tropaeolum speciosum*   Patriotism

12 *Salvia splendens* (Cleopatra Series)
   'Cleopatra Red'   I think of you

13 *Dahlia* 'Bishop of Llandaff'
   Good taste, instability

14 *Papaver commutatum*
   Fantastic extravagance

15 *Foeniculum vulgare* 'Purpureum'   Strength

16 *Osteospermum* 'White Pim'   Innocence

17 *Centaurea cyanus* (pink & white)   Delicacy

18 *Salvia officinalis* 'Purpurascens'
   Domestic virtue

19 *Nicotiana alata*   Peace

20 *Lantana montevidensis*   Rigor

above Designed by Edna Walling, a follower of Gertrude Jekyll, this Australian garden shows how effectively dividing a romantic garden into a series of experiences, each one designed to draw the visitor on, settles the tone.

right This Irish garden artlessly combines a flowering display that immediately whispers "romantic" in a seductive way, with a selection of plants that have a soft, rounded form that sets the visitor's eye and mood at ease—a floral feather mattress!

21 *Matthiola incana* Lasting beauty

22 *Camellia japonica* 'Jupiter'
   Unpretending excellence

23 *Rosa gallica* 'Versicolor' Variety

24 *Camellia japonica* 'Silver Anniversary'
   Perfected loveliness

25 *Reseda odorata* 'Grandiflora'
   Your qualities surpass your charms

26 *Lobularia maritima*
   Worth beyond beauty

27 *Cardiocrinum giganteum*
   Sweetness; modesty; purity

28 *Lilium* Golden Spendor Group
   Falsehood; gaiety

29 *Verbena laciniata* 'Lavender Mist'
   Pure; guileless

30 *Zinnia elegans* 'Desert Sun'
   Thoughts of an absent friend

31 *Alchemilla mollis* Fashion

32 *Arbutus unedo* Esteem (with love)

33 *Anethum graveolens* Good spirits

34 *Gladiolus* 'Victor Borge' Strong character

35 *Nigella damascena* 'Miss Jekyll'
   Perplexity

36 *Dimorphotheca pluvialis*
   Unconscious

37 *Fragaria vesca* 'Semperflorens'
   Perfect elegance

38 *Hibiscus syriacus* 'Diana'
   Delicate beauty

Planting scheme A

Rosa Alec's Red ('Cored') Passion; beauty

Rosa Paul Shirville ('Harqueterwife')
   Friendship; graceful beauty

Rosa Iceberg ('Korbin')
   Purity; the giver is worthy of your love

Planting scheme B

Dianthus 'Emile Paré' Boldness

Dianthus 'Brympton Red' Pure love

Dianthus 'Dad's Favourite' Talent

Dianthus 'Mrs Sinkins' Talent

Planting scheme C

Vinca minor Early friendship

Vinca minor f. *alba* Pleasant recollections

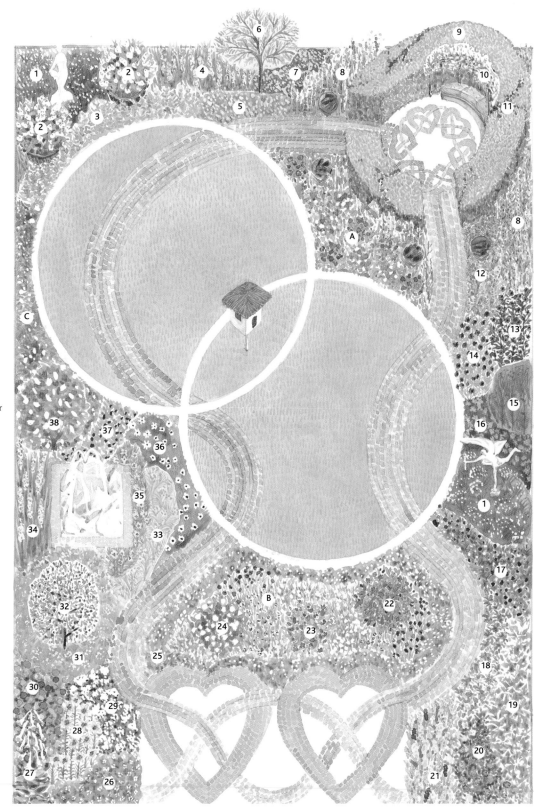

rural

The countryside—be it meadow, beach, or forest—has always exerted a strong influence on garden makers. Indeed, what is a cottage garden if it is not rural? It originated and evolved in the countryside, after all.

below Rural certainly does not equal dull, as this striking display of red candelabra primulas and *Primula vialii* shows. Moreover, a mix of exotics and natives can combine in a rurally inspired garden to create a "wild" look.

opposite This cottage garden in the French Alpes-Maritimes, with its roses and olive tree (*Olea europea*) is clearly a man-made, albeit untamed, interpretation of nature, but it melds seamlessly both with the rustic cottage and with the natural landscape that provides such a wonderfully dramatic backdrop.

The cottage garden shown in the plan on pages 58–59 is a deliberate attempt to capture the essence of a native countryside scene. Informally arranged, with no beginning and no end, the garden is intended to suggest an area that is carved out of a meadow, a natural scene, but one contrived so that it is not all visible at once, so a sense of mystery and surprise is retained.

Enclosure is provided by a white wooden fence and a hedgerow of native species. This not only provides a thick secure screen, it also encourages wildlife—a key aim of a native garden—and looks attractive all year round. In late spring and summer the wayfaring tree (*Viburnum lantana*), guelder rose (*Viburnum opulus*), dog rose, and sweetbriar (*Rosa canina* and *R. rubiginosa*) will flower. In fall and winter, the leaves of the field maple (*Acer campestre*) turn yellow, and berries appear on the spindle (*Euonymus europaeus*), hawthorn (*Crataegus monogyna*), and apple (*Malus prunifolia* 'Cheal's Crimson').

The boundary between hedgerow, bed, and path is blurred, so the areas flow naturally together, with the hedgerow underplanted with flowers. These also extend into the coarse grass on which progress around the garden is made. Whatever rural style you adopt, surfaces should be of natural materials to suit the scene. In this case wood chips, shredded bark, or rough cobbles are acceptable alternatives.

The only clearly man-made objects in the garden are the seating arrangements. A wooden bench girdles the English oak (*Quercus robur*) trunk, providing a relaxing and shady spot in summer. The nearby bee skep (an old type of hive) is of woven straw; unless you are a dedicated apiarist, it can be left simply as an ornament. Doubling up as a living sculpture and home to a

from the different species and broadcast them. Once established the plants will self-seed and become self-sustaining. The mixed species filling the bed nearest to the house have been deliberately selected to attract butterflies; their movement and color will introduce another dimension to the garden, whether viewed from within the house or when seated in the bower. Next to the pool, the bog garden is filled with brightly colored non-native primulas, although any combination of native moisture-loving plants would provide suitable alternatives for this area.

If a verdant hedgerow, wild flower meadow, and dew pond is not your ideal image of countryside, or will not suit your local conditions, remember that you are creating a cottage garden, and you can do what you like. You could import an interpretation of your local countryside, be this rolling hills, arid desert, prairie, veldt, heathland, or bush. Or you could be exotic and import someone else's—opt for a beach garden full of sand and coastal plants, a forest glade filled with trillium

Two distinctly different ways of creating a rural walk through an area of planting. In this Long Island garden (left) the design is wholly artificial, but the focal mulberry tree, the use of bark chippings to surface the path, and the informality of the colorful and exotic planting, dominated by *Lilium*, *Verbena bonariensis*, and *Imperata cylindrica* 'Rubra', imbues it with a rural feel. In contrast, the wildflower meadow at Great Dixter (below) deliberately and successfully sets out to replicate natural England, with the carefully integrated grass path causing minimal disturbance to the scene.

curvaceous wicker seat, the bower is constructed from live willow, which will come into leaf and provide shade in the summer when the air will also be perfumed by the honeysuckle flowers. And overhanging the pool—which is reminiscent of a dew pond, in which water collected for cattle to drink—is an area of wooden decking. (One word of caution when it comes to decking: please try to ensure that the wood you use comes from an environmentally sustainable source, rather than a nonrenewable one.) The deck is sufficiently large to accommodate a table and chairs, either placed under the protective shade of the Himalayan silver birch (*Betula utilis* var. *jacquemontii*) or right out over the pool. (Take care if you have children or young guests.) Its position and slight elevation offer the widest panorama of the garden, whether you are dining or relaxing in the hammock strung between two wooden poles. Uplighting the two large trees and the bower at night would introduce a mysterious glow to the scene after dusk.

The planting areas adjacent to the hedgerow are a random mix of native wildflowers—primarily annuals. To achieve the most natural look, mix together seeds

right This is the same Long
Island garden as opposite,
showing a wholly natural
foreground of wild carrot.
Taken together, the views
demonstrate that ingenious
design enables a very
successfull 'grading' of
rural scenery, from the
stylized to the imitation.

and other flora, or a Norwegian fjord with a rocky garden ending in a lake. The options are endless, limited only by your climate and studies of natural scenery.

When it comes to planting the countryside of your choice, another range of options opens up. The purist approach is to stick to those species that are native and indigenous to the particular scene being created; exactly copying the natural flora both in terms of species and of their natural associations will give you the most authentic look. However, as in the garden shown, it is possible to supplement this purity with other, non-native species that also thrive in these conditions and still achieve a natural look overall. Non-natives could be those escapees that have become naturalized (Dorothy Wordsworth spent a lot of her time scattering garden flower seed all over the Lake District!) or imports from other countries. At the other end of the scale, you can opt for a planting scheme that relies on any plant that will grow in your locale, whether it is native or not. This latter approach was the cornerstone of the perennial meadow that was developed in Germany by nurseryman Karl Foerster in the 1930s. His idea was to mass together large, informal drifts of relatively few species, through which emerged occasional clumps of taller species or the occasional shrub or small tree. This technique creates a very striking and natural display and is a very effective investment if you are gardening a large area and require maximum return for minimal input.

opposite This beautiful spring display is of moisture-loving plants including *Primula japonica*, *Hosta*, *Persicaria*, *Lysichiton americanus*, and *Euphorbia*, whose origins are all four corners of the globe. Yet it does not matter! A rural scene need not imitate immediate surroundings, but the planting should be informal, not formal.

above The use of rustic buildings, and if you are blessed with it, taking full advantage of a "borrowed" view over a natural landscape will help settle a rural garden, even to the extent that the planting within can be designed in a more stylized fashion.

left Another way to impart a rural feel is to work with the natural topography, as in this Welsh garden with its Welsh poppies, where the bridge heightens the glade feel. If you don't have nature on your side, you can manufacture your own with some judicious earth moving.

Plants for a rural garden

1 *Quercus robur*
2 *Betula utilis*
  var. *Jacquemontii*
3 *Salix triandra*
4 *Lonicera periclymenum*
  'Graham Thomas'

Planting scheme A
Acer campestre
Crataegus monogyna
Euonymus europaeus
Malus prunifolia
  'Cheal's Crimson'
Rosa canina
Rosa rubiginosa
Viburnum lantana
Viburnum opulus

Planting scheme B
Primula aureata
Primula burmanica
Primula prolifera
Primula pulverulenta
Primula sikkimensis
Primula vialii

Planting scheme C
Nymphaea 'Gonnère'
Nymphaea 'Oderata
  Sulphurea Grandiflora'

Planting scheme D
Agrostemma githago
Anthemis arvensis
Centaurea cyanus
Digitalis purpurea
Dipsacus fullonum
Leucanthemum vulgare
Lupinus polyphyllus
Malva moschata
Oenothera biennis
Papaver rhoeas
Xanthophthalmum segetum

Planting scheme E
Achillea millefolium
Centaurea nigra
Centaurea cyanus
Centaurea scabiosa
Knautia arvensis
Leucanthemum vulgare
Malva moschata

Planting scheme F
Longer growing grass
studded with the
following species:

Agrostemma githago
Anthemis arvensis
Centaurea cyanus
Digitalis purpurea
Dipsacus fullonum
Leucanthemum vulgare
Lupinus polyphyllus
Malva moschata
Oenothera biennis
Papaver rhoeas
Xanthophthalmum segetum

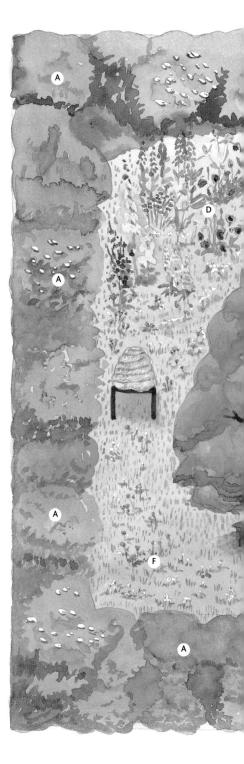

above An interesting
combination—a most un-rural
straight-line path is surfaced
with gravel, overhung by a
flowering *Cornus capitata*, and
lined with a mix of foxglove,
hardy geranium, and woodland
species. But it works, so never
be afraid to experiment, even
with the "un-natural."

formal

The cottage garden is not exclusively the realm of the informal. The mix of edible crops and old-fashioned plants can be a study in intricate geometry, symmetrical and asymmetrical, of straight and curved lines.

In my design, I have opted for straight lines and an arrangement of shapes and forms that gives the garden a geometrically formal look, while allowing convenient access to it (see the plan on pages 64–65). I have also used that most important and influential innovation of Italian Renaissance gardens—the main axis. A main axis is an ingenious design element that can be applied to a garden of any size. It is an invisible line that runs from the middle of the back wall of the house to infinity—you decide how far. In this case, it is the end wall. The axis is the hook from which the formal design hangs. Here, the garden on either side of the axis is a mirror image, although this need not always be the case: with

opposite In his own garden in Holland, Piet Oudolf uses hedges very effectively not just as a way of dividing the garden, but also as a way of introducing formal sculpture in a somewhat unusual way, thus adding to the garden's interesting form and structure.

above The neat low, clipped hedges of *Lonicera nitida*, together with the cone-shaped bay topiaries, give this Tasmanian cottage a formal setting, and help to blur the interface between the architecture and the garden.

both the Traditional (pages 28–29) and Modern designs (page 81), the layout is mirrored, but the plantings are not. Incidentally, these designs also use the concept of a "cross axis," a device that can be repeated and used to further subdivide the garden.

In addition to being an interesting pattern, which looks attractive when viewed from the upper rooms of the house, this garden benefits from a low-maintenance load and year-round structure, due to its significant use of hard landscaping and evergreen hedging.

Upon entering the garden, one's eye is drawn to the centrally positioned white limestone water feature. The arching jets and the gush of water from its pineapple-shaped fountainhead introduce sound and movement, while the fountain's curves contrast with the surrounding straight lines. Also in view, and positioned as a full stop or terminus to the main axis, as well as being the main feature in the further garden compartment, is an armillary sphere (a type of sundial) raised on a pedestal. Behind it are two angled mirror panels which create an eye-catching effect, both when viewed either at a distance or close up. Alternative main focal points appropriate to a formal cottage garden include classical statuary; abstract sculpture; a large, interestingly shaped rock (as used in traditional Chinese gardens) and perhaps drilled to convert it to a water feature; a well head; a seat (a vertical row boat partially sunk in the ground is an unusual option); or, for a larger space, a building or gazebo.

Four square, shallow canals occupy the corners of the garden compartment nearest the house, each crossed by a wooden bridge. The islands defined by the canals are planted with English yew (*Taxus baccata*), which is evergreen, clips very tightly, and here is grown as a formal, sculptural feature. Changes in height are used throughout the garden to introduce perspective and variety and to screen and frame specific vistas. The height of the yew cubes, through which the path passes, varies: those nearest to the house are half the size of those farther from it. And these taller cubes combine with the taller still yew "gatepost" flanking the path into the far garden compartment to block the line of sight, except for the gap where the canal runs. This vista offers a glimpse of what is beyond, generating a feeling of

surprise and anticipation, and drawing the visitor on, through to the far end of the garden.

Progress around the garden is by paths of water-washed cobbles, aligned in the direction of the path to encourage movement along them. Loose materials (such as sand, gravel, or stone chips) do not add to the level of intricate detail in the same way as solid, regularly shaped ones do, such as stone flags, reconstituted stone slabs, tiles, granite setts, or brick, whose inherent shape and the configuration pattern in which they are laid can be used to introduce form, pattern, and shape to the layout.

In terms of the ornamental planting, the chamomile lawns pick up the theme of a green "room." Depending on the prevailing climate, it will be semi- or evergreen and it releases its perfume into the air when walked on. The wildflower mix introduces a random touch to the formality and will produce a spectacular summer display as well as attracting butterflies and other wildlife into the garden, and the exact species mix should reflect the garden's geographic location. For a longer season of floral interest, plant the beds with seasonal bedding; for example, with Universal pansies for the winter (in temperate zones), and with bulbs (such as hyacinths, narcissi, and tulips) for the spring, and in summer, brightly coloured, tender exotics planted in masses, either in geometrical patterns or informal drifts.

A variation step would be to introduce "carpet bedding." This 19th-century innovation uses low-growing succulents and exotics with colored foliage planted closely together to create a "picture." Originally, coats of arms and zoomorphic displays were popular subjects, but abstract or geometric patterns would work very well in a formal cottage garden. Slope the beds (like a book rest) to make the pattern more obvious.

In contrast with the compartment nearest to the house, the distant rectangular green "room" is predominantly functional. The sward offers a space for children to play games (the surrounding planting is pretty resilient to ball damage), and there is plenty of space for a hammock in a frame or an easy chair in which to relax; there is also room to install garden furniture and a barbecue, and host a party. If a lawn is not required, however, you could extend the cobbles

opposite top Two varieties of box, clipped into neat hedges of the same proportion, bring feelings of order, variety, contrast, and harmony to this Australian ornamental vegetable garden. The empty gap between the two hedges is an especially attractive, but perhaps accidental, touch.

opposite centre In a very small garden it is much easier and often more satisfactory to opt for a formal layout rather than an informal one. Within a geometric layout, use plants to soften straight lines and introduce a note of contrasting informality.

opposite bottom Formal garden structures and buildings, especially when architecturally rather than rustically designed and positioned at the terminus of a walk or vista, sound a formal note, and can be used to echo the architecture of the house.

right This arrangement is given formality by a mix of controlled living plants—pleached trees, clipped hedges, lawn—and inanimate objects—tubular trellis, rectangular paving slabs, steps. The whole is moderated to perfection by the unbridled planting, which includes a white climbing rose, craning *Agapanthus*, feathery *Alchemilla mollis*, and architectural *Acanthus spinosus*.

into this part of the garden to provide continuity, or use another hard surface for variety. The planting is restricted to a perimeter border containing informal drifts of ornamental grasses. Grasses offer so much over a long season of interest; they are fresh looking when juvenile; they look great all summer; some also offer autumnal foliage and seed-head display (nature's bird food); and all look stunning when cloaked by a hoarfrost. Moreover, they require little maintenance, while their verdant tones are calming on the eye.

However, if you are aiming for more formal planting than a selection of grasses offers, then a knot garden aligned on the main axis (either a single large knot or a set of three), or an arrangement of beds, perhaps raised for vertical interest, would be perfect alternatives.

left "Keep it simple" is a wise axiom to bear in mind when designing formally. In a Californian garden the plain straight lines of the bed edge, path, hedge, and beautifully constructed wall draw the visitor to the gate and into another part of the garden.

above The ethos "less is more" also governs this Suffolk garden. A geometric but uncomplicated pattern of the knot bed is set within a sea of gravel that wonderfully sets off the large pithos and its silver dreadlocks.

Plants for a formal garden

1 *Phyllostachys aureosulcata*
  f. *aureocaulis*
2 *Cortaderia selloana* 'Silver Comet'
3 *Briza maxima*
4 *Carex elata* 'Aurea'
5 *Festuca glauca*

6 *Miscanthus sinensis* 'Gracillimus'
7 *Stipa calamagrostis*
8 *Hakonechloa macra* 'Aureola'
9 *Taxus baccata*
10 *Tropaeolum speciosum*
11 *Chamaemelum nobile*

Planting scheme A
Agrostemma githago
Anthemis arvensis
Centaurea cyanus
Digitalis purpurea
Dipsacus fullonum

Leucanthemum vulgare
Lupinus polyphyllus
Malva moschata
Oenothera biennis
Papaver rhoeas
Xanthophthalmum segetum

painterly

Artists such as Impressionist painter Claude Monet,
garden designer Gertrude Jekyll, and writer Vita Sackville-
West were innovators in the way they applied the
color theory of fine art to their gardens, combined with
the time-honored techniques of the craftsman.

opposite A white fence and brick walls form a mellow stage canvas on which the display of *Rosa* 'Ballerina' and her accompanying delphiniums take center stage. Anchored by the greens of the foliage, the display runs an harmonious scale from deep violet through mauve to pale pink and red.

left This long herbaceous border at Egeskov Slotshave in Denmark comprehensively demonstrates that a well-designed show owes as much to plant form and height as it does flowering color. On this large scale, the rewards of planting in large drifts or clumps are easily seen.

At her garden at Sissinghurst in Kent, Vita Sackville-West popularized the concept of monochrome planting displays, the White Garden being her most famous creation. Monet used the long borders in his garden at Giverny in France as a "laboratory," where he experimented with color combinations, and the water lily lake he created was the subject of some of his most famous works. But Miss Jekyll was the first to take the concept of painterly color theory and apply it to beds and borders—by using plants to paint garden pictures. Thus was born a new type of cottage garden that drew on the finest of the past, but in which edible crops were replaced by a display of hardy plants arranged to best show off their individual beauty and to unite together in a carefully color-coordinated display.

Today there are many different ways in which art can be used to inspire a cottage garden. It would be possible to take a painting of an old-fashioned cottage garden and set out to recreate an authentic look. Alternatively, the garden can become the frame for a set of sculptural pieces, such as Barbara Hepworth's garden in St. Ives, Cornwall. Or inspiration can be drawn from the way that painters such as Pablo Picasso, Paul Klee, or Henri Matisse used color and form. I am a great devotee of both Miss Jekyll's work and that of the Modernists, and in this garden I have attempted to meld together the styles of these unlikely bedfellows. The central layout is based loosely on a white artwork by the English artist Ben Nicholson, which is composed of pieces of shaped card stock glued on top of one another. A similar work was made into a sculpture and used as a focal point to be reflected in a rectangular pool in the garden at Sutton

Place, designed by Nicholson's friend, the landscape architect Sir Geoffrey Jellicoe. Here the garden layout mirrors the different parts of the artwork. When it came to dealing with these separate areas, I also took my inspiration from the linear works of Dutch abstract painter Piet Mondrian, in which he used strongly contrasting monochrome blocks of color.

The garden is enclosed by a whitewashed brick wall, which acts as a plain frame for the garden art (as does the card edging for Nicholson's work). One enters the garden across the expanse of the sky-blue canal,

above These dark rose-red hollyhocks are a piece of art in their own right; so always take an holistic approach to every plant: Consider its height and spread, foliage form and color, and its flowering color and time. And remember that individual specimens or small clumps can be used as pieces of art in their own right.

above In this Connecticut garden, the flame-orange flower and large red and brown striped leaves of the *Canna* harmonize with its yellow and green cousin, the adjacent *Rudbeckia*, and background *Cotinus coggygria*, yet it is so powerful that it has an individual impact almost like an exclamation mark!

right The "hot" mid-section of Miss Jekyll's famous Long Border was originally planted in her garden at Munstead Wood, and is here recreated in the Botanic Garden at Reading University, where it features *Dahlia*, *Celosia*, *Tagetes*, *Canna*, and *Helianthus*. Miss Jekyll developed the concept, and has yet to be bettered.

left A much under-used but very effective device when devising planting schemes is repetition. Repeating groups of the same plant in several places within a scheme, such as the gladioli in this border, brings balance and harmony and helps to unify the whole.

almost as if one is crossing a moat. The fountains introduce dynamism and the sound of moving water, and the stepping stones lead to the central seating area, where the pattern of the granite setts shows the whole garden layout in miniature.

Changes in level are introduced by circular raised and sunken beds. All make use of mass plantings of the same plant to create a bold color statement. In the former, the blue of the *Lavandula stoechas* picks up on the color of the canal and together with the expanse of fine green sward, crowned with an architecturally trained form of an *Acer palmatum* var. *dissectum* planted within a green glazed Japanese pot, serves as a foil to the hot colors of the sunken bed. Here, the deep purple foliage of the *Cotinus coggygria* 'Notcutt's Variety' (which should be cut to the ground every winter to ensure it produces large juvenile leaves) has echoes of the Japanese maple, and harmonizes with the hot deep-red flowers and foliage of *Lobelia* 'Queen Victoria' (which thanks to the depth of the sunken bed creates a carpetlike effect when viewed at ground level.) The reds give way to the warm yellow of *Osteospermum* 'Buttermilk', which, in turn, contrasts with the blues of the canal and the lavender.

Surrounding the Mondrian/Nicholson-inspired areas is an herbaceous border, its color scheme influenced by the Long Border that Miss Jekyll created in her garden at Munstead Wood, in Surrey. The color scheme begins in the bottom left corner with yellows, blues, and whites. Then, as the bed is slightly raised, these blur into the cooler yellows and whites before turning the corner to the far border, where the colors warm up into the yellows then the hot reds and oranges (the hot colors drawing the eye to the garden's end and contrasting with the central lawn), before the colours cool again down the right-hand border, where yellows and white merge into blues and whites. This possibly is an attempt to squeeze a quart into a pint pot, but the idea of going from cool colors through warm ones to the focal point of hot ones, and then cooling down again is very pleasing on the eye and helps create a very harmonious atmosphere. Color co-ordination need not include the whole spectrum, however. Foliage color as well as flowers can be most effectively used in monochrome borders of red or blue,

left It need not only be about bright flowers. Foliage form and color—such as that of the *Rodgersia aesculifolia*, *Iris pseudacorus* 'Variegata', *Hakonechloa macra* 'Aureola , and *Hosta* (Tardiana Group) 'Wedgwood' in this planting group—can be most effectively used to create a most calming effect, which can be highlighted by the occasional flower, such as the *Geranium psilostemon* peeping through at the back. This is a most useful approach in shady corners.

below left Christopher Lloyd has a well-deserved reputation as an expert plant designer, and in recent years he has turned his skills to creating exotic displays such as this unlikely but effective combination of *Canna*, asters, nasturtium and *Crocosmia*.

and it is often overlooked that Sissinghurst's White Garden is as dependent for its effect on the foliage greens included in the display as it is on the signature white flowers. Displays using only a couple of harmonizing (or contrasting) colors also work very well —for example, a spring garden of whites and yellows, or a summer border that includes only reds and yellows, or blues and yellows.

However, the successful application of color theory to gardens is difficult, for one is dealing with a material that has many dimensions, all of which have to be taken into consideration at the same time. A plant has a height, a spread, and an overall form (shape). Add to this the texture, shape, and color of the foliage and the shape and color and flowering time of the flowers, and you start to realize that a successful color-coordinated bed or border—particularly on a large scale—is an art form in its own right, and something that is achieved only with practice. So do not fret if it takes you a few attempts. Part of the joy of the process of gardening is learning from your mistakes, which are always easy to rectify, after all. It is not so hard to dig up a plant or two and replace them with something else.

opposite This summer border at Chateau de Pontrancart in France shows just how effective a monochrome display, based on tints and tones of a single color, can be, and just how much the flower forms play a role in the overall display.

left Red is an immediate color, drawing the eye straight to it; and one of the most beautiful of all red flowers is *Dahlia* 'Bishop of Llandaff'. Here the spindly *Verbena bonariensis* provides an interesting contrast in form, while its flowers complement the Bishop's foliage.

Plants for a painterly garden

1 *Rudbeckia fulgida* var. *speciosa*
2 *Lilium lancifolium*
3 *Dahlia* 'Hamari Accord'
4 *Hemerocallis citrina*
5 *Tagetes erecta*
6 *Dahlia* 'Bishop of Llandaff'
7 *Gypsophila paniculata* 'Bristol Fairy'
8 *Canna indica* (orange)
9 *Tropaeolum majus* (orange)
10 *Alcea rosea* (deep red)
11 *Kniphofia* 'Royal Standard'
12 *Canna indica* (red)
13 *Celosia argentea* (Olympia Series) 'Olympia Red'
14 *Helianthus* x *multiflorus*
15 *Lychnis chalcedonica*
16 *Salvia* x *superba*
17 *Kniphofia galpinii* (dwarf)
18 *Antirrhinum majus* (tall yellow)
19 *Eryngium giganteum*
20 *Lilium monadelphum*
21 *Eryngium* x *oliverianum*
22 *Lathyrus latifolius* 'White Pearl'
23 *Iris pallida* subsp. *pallida*
24 *Verbascum bombyciferum*
25 *Crambe maritima*
26 *Delphinium* (Belladonna Group) 'Cliveden Beauty'
27 *Senecio cineraria*
28 *Alcea rosea* (sulphur yellow)
29 *Dictamnus albus*
30 *Yucca filamentosa*
31 *Phlox paniculata* 'Balmoral'
32 *Lilium* 'Bright Star'
33 *Antirrhinum majus* (tall white)
34 *Veronica spicata* 'Romiley Purple'
35 *Santolina chamaecyparissus*
36 *Geranium ibericum*
37 *Ruta graveolens*
38 *Campanula lactiflora*
39 *Stachys byzantina*
40 *Dahlia* 'White Moonlight'
41 *Achillea* 'Coronation Gold'
42 *Coreopsis lanceolata*
43 *Bergenia cordifolia*
44 *Iris orientalis*
45 *Monarda didyma*
46 *Smyrnium perfoliatum*

above It is almost impossible to go wrong with any combination of the prime colors, while white (and very pale pastel shades) brings a touch of calm to any planting display, as demonstrated here by the *Kniphofia*, *Achillea*, *Dahlia*, *Salvia*, and *Delphinium*, and soothing *Philadelphus*.

color as it can make the light beneath the awning very unpleasant. The second living space is a sunken seat. Steps, also reached by the concrete path, descend to the gray slate floor and the contrasting white marble bench running around the edge. Around the perimeter, the glass nuggets echo the path edging, and a hedge of *Lavandula angustifolia* 'Hidcote' increases privacy and introduces a sweet smell to the seat. The seating area could have additional avant-garde furniture or be floored with colored rubber sheeting or etched and uplit glass. The planting surrounding the dining area and sunken seat is a scatter of traditional annuals and herbs as a reminder of this garden's antecedents, although these could be exchanged for perennials or a bold display of bedding plants. For lower maintenance, plant shrubs and perennials.

The focal points of the garden are the centrally positioned fire cube and the glass water slide. The cross paths leading from the fire pool terminate in twin stainless-steel pergolas, smothered with white jasmine, which provide a setting for a pair of abstract sculptures. Backing any three-dimensional artwork with mirrors allows the reverse to be seen and introduces an optical illusion of increased size. Possible alternative features include murals, metal artworks, vases with water pouring over the rim, and glass sculptures. The fire cube is made of polished gray slate, on top of which sits a deep-rimmed carved-slate bowl, the source of jets of flame (supplied by a gas bottle hidden within the cube). The cube is set within a white marble-lined pool, which has contrasting jets of water rising from it. Both materials pick up on those used in the sunken seating area. The water slide terminating the garden is positioned on the main axis and is a backdrop to the fire cube. The sand-blasted glass surface (colored glass is another option) is raised in a fish-scale pattern, causing the water to jump as it moves down, glittering in sunlight and introducing dynamism and movement to the overall design. This feature could also be uplit at night using fiber-optic lighting to make it glow.

left All fashions now accepted as "establishment" were once modern, and so it is beholden on today's garden makers to be thought provoking, controversial, and to push the boundaries. And in the process beautiful gardens, such as this amalgam of art and nature, organic and man-made, will emerge to inspire.

above Plants as architecture: The combination of the *Canna*, *Abutilon* and *Arundo donax* var. *versicolor* is a very effective way in which a resourceful designer can simultaneously complement and enhance a modern garden structure, introduce a new set of characteristics, and develop a unified garden that is anchored to its setting and house.

Plants for a modern garden

1 *Lavandula angustifolia* 'Hidcote'
2 *Allium giganteum*
3 *Matthiola incana* Brompton Group, mixed
4 *Freesia* Super Giant Series, mixed
5 *Lilium regale*
6 *Cynara cardunculus*
7 *Helianthus annuus* (red)
8 *Rudbeckia fulgida* var. *speciosa*
9 *Jasminum officinale*
10 Lettuce 'Lollo Rossa' (*Lactuca sativa*)
11 Lettuce (green) (*Lactuca sativa*)
12 Carrot (*Daucus carota*)
13 Pea (*Pisum sativum*)
14 Runner bean (white flowered)
   (*Phaseolus coccineus*)
15 Lablab bean (*Lablab purpureus*)
16 Asparagus (*Asparagus officinalis*)

Planting scheme A

Allium schoenoprasum
Antirrhinum majus (mixed)
Centaurea cyanus (blue, pink, & white)
Consolida ajacis (dwarf)
Dianthus barbatus
Foeniculum vulgare
Lavandula stoechas
Lychnis flos-jovis
Mentha spicata
Matthiola longipetala subsp. *bicornis*
Myosotis sylvatica
Nigella damascena
Ocimum basilicum
Papaver commutatum
Petroselinum crispum
Rosmarinus officinale
Salvia officinalis
Scabiosa atropurpurea
Tagetes erecta

designing by
use

aromatic

The sense of smell is perhaps the most underestimated of the senses, but it produces the strongest emotional response—the scent of certain flowers will always take us back to childhood or trigger a special memory.

below It's raining flowers. Taking a seat on this particular garden bench beneath such a torrential downpour of wisteria could result in serious olfactory overload. Alongside or over any path is the perfect setting to get the most from a display of scented plants.

right *Rosa* 'Constance Spry' was one of David Austin's earliest creations (1961), and was named after the famous flower arranger who had done so much to save old-fashioned rose varieties when they fell from fashion in the 1920s.

Moreover, sweetly smelling plants are a great aid to creating a garden atmosphere conducive to relaxing—a sort of nature's own aromatherapy. The aim of this aromatic cottage garden is to create just such a scented haven, in which to retreat from the hustle and bustle of the outside world and revivify the mind and body. The living space is therefore positioned in the middle of the garden, with as much scented planting around it as possible to maximize the nasal impact.

Indeed, the planting scheme focuses on those plants that have scented flowers that give their perfume freely, releasing it into the air, rather than those with scented foliage which require the leaves to be bruised before they will give up their scent. This latter form of aromatic garden can easily be created, too, especially if you focus on herb species and plant them in positions where visitors will readily brush against them.

There are two scented retreats: the first, nearest the house, is easily reached by the path from the back door, which is framed by two "sentinel" *Yucca whipplei*. These introduce all-year form, and their greenish-white, bell-shaped flowers, which appear in late spring, are deliciously lemon-scented. This nearer space is designed for daytime use, and it is covered by a wooden pergola (one with brick piers would work equally well), which is smothered with sweetly smelling flowering climbers (jasmine, wisteria, honeysuckle and an early-flowering climbing rose). Together, the support and plants combine to produce a shady, scented retreat. As always, personal taste should, and has, dictated the planting selection, and in this case the bouquet of perfumes is enriched further by the adjacent plantings of roses, lilies, and freesias. However, there are many other summer-flowering plants that offer equally rich fragrance, and to increase the seasonal use of the garden, you could introduce scented winter- and spring-flowering shrubs, such as witch hazel, mahonia, *Lonicera fragrantissima*, and *Chimonanthus praecox*. This last also trains well, and planted against a sheltered, south-facing wall, it will help create a lovely scented spot on a warm, winter day.

This retreat is the perfect place to set a couple of stone benches or a reclining chair and while away the scented hours with a delicious alfresco lunch, followed by a long snooze or a good book. Then, as the sun begins to set, it is time to move into the farther retreat. Paved with the same rounded stone flags, in order to introduce

right Raising this bed with a brick wall links it to the house, draws attention to the visual display of roses, including *Rosa* 'Raubritter', and brings them closer to nose height so that their scent has a greater impact.

left The foliage greens and purple flowers of the *Verbena bonariensis*, *Petunia*, and heliotrope set off one another, and on a warm day this last will perfume the air with its rich honey scent, a magnet for bees.

opposite above Embraced by a bed of cat nip (*Nepeta*), this rustic bench looks out over the vari-colored mounds of a thyme bed. Having paths lined with fragrant herbs is another way to perfume the air, which happens every time someone brushes past their leaves.

opposite below This composition is a close-up of the outside of the famous laburnum walk created at Barnsley House in Gloucestershire by the late, great Rosemary Verey, with wisteria and *Allium hollandicum* in the foreground.

harmony (the gaps between which could be planted with low-growing herbs such as chamomile and wild thyme to release a fragrance when stepped upon), this retreat is primarily bounded with flowering plants. These give off their perfume at dusk, thus also making this the perfect place to entertain in the evening. The plants chosen are also primarily white-flowered, introducing an ethereal glow to the surroundings at twilight.

There is deliberately no direct access from the nearer to the farther garden "room." The aim is to require the visitor to walk along the path and to increase the olfactory experience. An exception to the no-aromatic-foliage-planting approach outlined above is the lavender hedge, which lines both sides of the path. Although I could argue that I selected it for its flowers, it is the foliage that introduces an evergreen structure to the garden and that releases the sweetest perfume when brushed against. Low hedges of scented foliage can also be made from lavender cotton (*Santolina chamaecyparissus*),

hyssop (*Hyssopus officinalis*), or, for a more informal hedge, rosemary (*Rosmarinus officinalis*). More scent will arise from both the path itself, which is surfaced with shredded pine, which releases a heady, resinous aroma, especially in hot weather (the perfect accompaniment to a chilled bottle of Greek retsina enjoyed under the pergola), and the adjacent planting. The long borders flanking the paths are planted in true cottage-garden tradition with a random mix of scented annuals, while near the house the planting of soft blues, yellows, whites and pinks harmonizes with the lavender hedge and a collection of traditional roses in pinks, whites, and reds. The soft tones of the roses complements their scent, as an aid to relaxation, while their form only slightly screens the seating area, defining it, but welcoming the visitor.

The twin lemon trees, in ornate terracotta pots placed between the retreats, are eye-catchers; they help to create a physical and visual barrier between the two areas. If frost is not an issue, plant citrus into the beds, and supplement them with tender scented plants such as *Gardenia*, *Hedychium* and *Plumeria* and, for the walls *Jasminum polyanthum* with *Trachelospermum jasminoides*. In this case, climbers are also used to introduce additional scent: the deep pink-flowered *Rosa* 'Zéphirine

Drouhin' is mixed with multicolored sweet peas at the end of the garden. Other great scented climbing roses include the yellow *R.* 'Maigold' (used on the pergola), the creamy-white *R.* 'Madame Alfred Carrière' and *R.* 'Gloire de Dijon', the pink *R.* 'Aloha', and the dark red *R.* 'Guinée'. To make a visual statement, my favorite scented climber, jasmine, runs along wires the length of both side walls.

The primary aim of the garden is to create a space to relax, based around sweet scents, complemented by soft flower colors. But to complete the relaxing sensory experience, water is essential. The visual barrier between the retreats is lowered around the three-tiered bowl fountain, which is set in a carpet of the old-fashioned *Dianthus* 'Musgrave's Pink'. This allows the fountain, which brings gentle movement and soothing sound, to be a focal point the moment one enters the garden, thus drawing the visitor toward it. Visible from both retreats, it helps create a unity between them, while each retains its individuality. I think the sound and sight of water are exceptional aids to relaxing in a garden, but if a tall fountain is too much, a bowl sunk into the paving at ground level with a low fountain, a bubbler appearing from the hole in a millstone, or even a small wall-mounted fountain, would be appropriate.

above The regal lily (*Lilium regale*) is one of the most beautiful and sweetly scented of all lilies. It was discovered by Ernest Wilson, and a massed planting such as this must give a sense of how the whole Chinese valley must have smelled when he first came across it in 1903.

above This small border in a Tasmanian garden is so understated but so effective. Flanked by two sentinel topiary bay trees and enclosed by *Lonicera nitida*, the path is edged with golden marjoram and the border filled with *Gaura lindheimeri*.

Plants for an aromatic garden

1 *Hedychium gardnerianum*
2 *Dictamnus albus* (white)
3 *Hesperis matronalis* var. *albiflora*
4 *Nicotiana sylvestris*
5 *Matthiola longipetala* subsp.
   bicornis
6 *Matthiola incana*
   Cinderella Series, mixed
7 *Freesia* (mixed) 8 *Rosa moschata*
9 *Hedychium coronarium*
10 *Lavandula angustifolia* 'Hidcote'
11 *Jasminum officinale*
12 *Lilium martagon*
13 *Nicotiana alata*
14 *Lilium regale*
15 *Citrus limon*
16 *Dianthus* 'Musgrave's Pink'
17 *Lilium monadelphum*
18 *Wisteria sinensis* 'Alba'
19 *Lonicera periclymenum*
   'Graham Thomas'
20 *Rosa* 'Maigold'
21 *Wisteria sinensis*
22 *Rosa* 'Indigo'
23 *Rosa* x *alba*
24 *Rosa gallica* 'Versicolor'
25 *Rosa* 'Constance Spry'
26 *Rosa* 'Madame Isaac Pereire'
27 *Hesperis matronalis*
28 *Dictamnus albus* (pink)
29 *Heliotropium arborescens*
30 *Yucca whipplei*
31 *Dianthus* 'Fenbow Nutmeg Clove'
32 *Rosa hemisphaerica*

Planting scheme A

Lathyrus odoratus (mixed)
Rosa 'Zéphirine Drouhin'

Planting scheme B

Dianthus barbatus (mixed)
Iberis amara
Nicotiana x *sanderae*
   Domino Series, mixed
Reseda odorata 'Grandiflora'
Zaluzianskya capensis

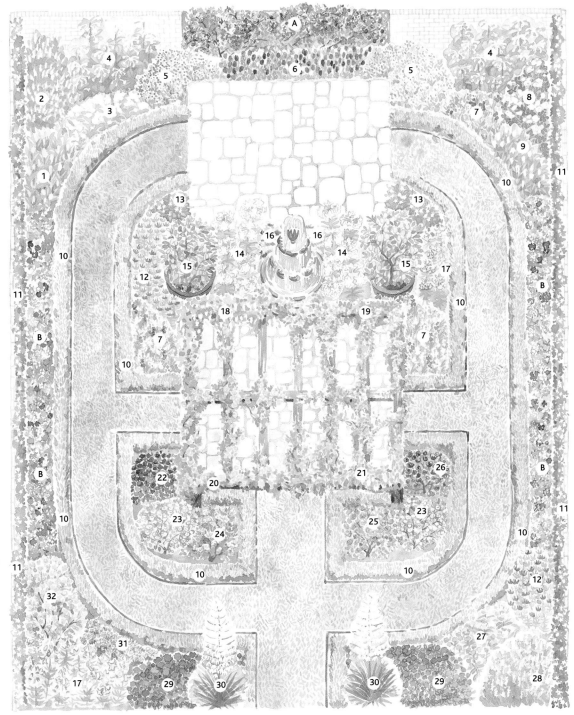

wildlife

Even the average garden is now recognized as an important wildlife refuge. But by specifically creating a wildlife garden, you can make an even greater contribution to the survival of the flora and fauna indigenous to your area.

left In her woodland garden in Essex, Beth Chatto has integrated ferns, ornamental shrubs, and perennials such as *Mahonia*, *Hosta*, *Aquilegia*, *Doronicum*, and *Romneya coulteri* within a wild setting, resulting in an "improved nature" every bit as beautiful as it is wildlife friendly.

above July in this wildflower meadow garden is dominated by an unseasonable snow-like setting of ox-eye daisies for the natural monolith and man-made mirror stellae, with their echoes of ancient civilizations.

Besides facilitating the "feel-good" factor of helping preserve the environment, wildlife gardens can be very eye-catching in their own right. They serve as an excellent educational tool for children, and offer much fun and excitement: watching the garden and keeping a wildlife diary; recording the flowering times and success (or not) of the flora; and monitoring the visits of the different birds, insects, mammals, and amphibians that will be drawn into your cottage wildlife garden.

The key to creating a successful wildlife garden is to attract local, indigenous fauna. Thus, the garden should be planted with those species that attract such wildlife. Most plants, therefore, will also be native, but not

necessarily all—for example, the butterfly bush (*Buddleja davidii*), widely grown in British gardens to attract butterflies, is native to Japan. But there is more to creating a wildlife garden than simply pulling a few names from a book of native plants—it is essential to consider the needs of the wildlife that you wish to attract. All forms of wildlife have two basic requirements for life: shelter and food (although, of course, different types of creature have different specific requirements). Therefore, to maximize the success of your wildlife garden, it is necessary to understand the creatures' needs and to create a range of habitats to meet them. A good starting point is to do a bit of research. Contact your local wildlife society or community wildlife projects, or take a look on the Internet to discover both what fauna can be encouraged into your garden and which plants will be of most benefit to them.

Clearly, the specific contents of a successful wildlife garden depend on the location. However, there are some guidelines that apply to all wildlife gardens, and the plan on pages 98–99 shows a garden that, while specifically planted to attract Northern European fauna, covers these basics.

Enclosed by a woven willow fence, the layout is intended to be very informal and naturalistic, but to look attractive and be functional, while still containing as wide a range of habitats as the space allows. From the house, an oak-plank bridge crosses the pool to a

above A bog garden at the interface between a pool and dry land offers another habitat, providing protection and food for amphibians and insects. It also presents the chance to grow ornamental plants, such as this striking moisture-loving Iris in a New Zealand garden.

right The genus *Nymphaea* contains both hardy and tender species (which can be grown in a greenhouse pool in cold climes); they are essential for the success of a wildlife pond, shading and keeping the water cool (and rich in oxygen) in summer and giving protection to fish and amphibians.

opposite Okay, it's a bit more than a cottage garden, but the point is that a wildlife cottage garden, as well as providing a refuge and food for indigenous fauna, and thus aiding its conservation, can be a visually stunning and calm spot filled with common-place and exotic plants, such as ferns, *Gunnera*, sedges, and skunk cabbage.

wooden-framed summerhouse thatched with reeds and open at the sides; from here, the wildlife can be watched, or one can simply relax. Behind is a rough meadow, which has been studded with wildflowers to look attractive, but it is also a place where a table and chairs could be placed for entertaining or for playing games.

Providing water is great way to attract wildlife and even a simple birdbath will work, but to maximize the potential, a large pond is the answer (however, if you have small children, you may want to think twice, as kids and deep water are not a wise mix.) A pond should be a minimum of 3ft (90cm), and preferably 4ft (120cm) deep, have a gently sloping edge and shallow margins so that toads, frogs, birds, and insects can get in and out, and within the pool, it should increase in depth in a series of 1ft (30cm) steps so that there are different depths to accommodate different water plants. To keep

the water cool, it should have approximately 50 percent cover from aquatic plants such as waterlilies. Install a small fountain (even one of the floating, solar-powered ones will do the trick) to help oxygenate the water—the sound of moving water will also attract birds and other wildlife, but do not have a huge jet, for the water disturbance it causes will deter wildlife. Juxtaposed with the pool is a bog garden planted with native plants, which sets off the pool aesthetically and creates a pretty scene, but also provides a safe refuge and food for amphibians and other wildlife that live near water.

The areas around the periphery of the garden are not to be used as a recreational area, but rather left undisturbed for the wildlife. The mix of annuals, perennials, and shrubs is one that will attract butterflies and provide food and shelter for birds. Like most gardeners, butterflies like warm and sheltered

above The Dutch master of creating a stylized perennial meadow look, Piet Oudolf is at his finest in a Norfolk garden. Large drifts of herbaceous perennials, including *Liatris*, *Monarda*, and *Astilbe* rub shoulders with ornamental grasses in a carefully contrived display of color and form.

below The natural-look, wildlife garden works on the grand scale as shown left, but it is equally stunning in detail, as a vignette from the spring meadow at Great Dixter in Sussex demonstrates. The nodding heads of the purple and white forms of *Fritillaria meleagris* look down on the starry white *Anemone nemorosa*, while the cheerfully yellow *Narcissus* stands guard.

right A wildlife garden should not just be about attracting the flying, hopping, crawling, and slithering creatures. Many indigenous plants around the world are also threatened, so if your soil allows (and most wildflowers usually thrive on very poor soil), make part of your garden a plant refuge. This *Dactylorhiza* orchid thrives in a Normandy garden.

conditions, so pick a sunny spot for your butterfly garden. Butterflies also need minerals, that can be obtained from manure or damp soil, and some also feed on rotting fruit or vegetation. A compost pile is an ideal addition to your wildlifegarden, as it not only helps out the butterfly population but also acts as a source of food and shelter. Insects and invertebrates will be found there, and these, in turn, form part of the diet of useful invertebrates, notably worms, and mammals. Another way to help maximise the number of butterflies is to plant a range of plant species that caterpillars can feed on. Butterflies have very specific needs, so again research which plant species are the best hosts for larvae.

Birds need shelter to rest, sleep, and nest, and they need food and water. Ideally, depending on its size, a wildlife garden should contain either a hedgerow or a small thicket, or preferably both. In this example, there is a copse of woodland trees to which bird boxes could be attached. Shrubs provide a range of nesting and roosting spots and a greater diversity of food, both in terms of plant seeds and berries and of the range of food insects attracted to the plants. Indeed, the English oak (*Quercus robur*) is home to several hundred insect species; the sycamore (*Acer pseudoplatanus*), only to two. Bird feeders are another worthwhile addition. Rotting

tree trunks provide a habitat for many insects and invertebrates, as well as being an interesting feature. And if they become colonized by fungi, the autumnal display can be spectacular. Another habitat that would provide shelter to larger wildlife species, such as newts and frogs, is a pile of rocks—but remember to leave empty spaces underneath the stones.

Finally, and at the risk of pointing out the obvious, if you have a wildlife garden, you should garden organically and never use any chemical sprays – but should you feel the need to kill there are many organic alternatives now available. If you get the planting right, your wildlife garden will be its own sustainable ecosystem, in which the gardener's pests become dinner for other animals. And don't forget that the aim of wildlife gardening is to attract wildlife, not to have every plant looking exhibition-perfect.

right Cottage garden meets wildlife: A lovely higgledy-piggledy mixture of different colored *Iris*, ox-eye daisy, and honesty (*Lunaria*).

below This wildlife garden in France has a distinctly Far Eastern feel about it, with the stream-side planting dominated by plants indigenous to China and Japan: *Hosta*, candelabra primulas, and a striking pink-red Chinese rose. Yet, despite their foreign provenance these introductions will help encourage a wildlife community.

Plants for a wildlife garden

1 *Malus prunifolia* 'Cheal's Crimson'
2 *Ilex aquifolium*
3 *Acer campestre*
4 *Crataegus monogyna*
5 *Quercus robur*
6 *Euonymus europaeus*
7 *Buddleja alternifolia*
8 *Rosa rugosa*
9 *Viburnum opulus*
10 *Buddleja davidii* 'Black Knight'

Planting scheme A

Campanula trachelium
Chelidonium majus
Digitalis purpurea
Fragaria vesca
Lamium galeobdolon
Myosotis sylvatica
Primula vulgaris
Silene dioica
Teucrium scorodonia

Planting scheme B

Centaurea maculosa
Galium verum
Knautia arvensis
Leucanthemum vulgare
Lotus corniculatus
Ranunculus bulbosus
Primula veris
Trifolium pratense
Vicia cracca

Planting scheme C

Nymphaea odorata
Nymphaea odorata var. *rosea*

Planting scheme D

Anagallis tenella
Caltha palustris
Cardamine pratensis
Eupatorium cannabinum
Filipendula ulmaria
Geum rivale
Iris pseudacorus

Lychnis flos-cuculi
Lycopus europaeus
Lysimachia nummularia
Lythrum salicaria
Pulicaria dysenterica
Stachys palustris

Planting scheme E

Anthyllis vulneraria
Aruncus dioicus
Centranthus ruber
Centaurea scabiosa
Centaurea nigra

Dipsacus fullonum
Eupatorium cannabinum
Hypochaeris radicata
Knautia arvensis
Leucanthemum vulgare
Lotus corniculatus

Lythrum salicaria
Rumex acetosa
Sanguisorba officinalis
Scabiosa columbaria
Succisa pratensis

herbal

Herbs have always been an intrinsic part of the cottage garden planting ethos. They not only are attractive, they also have numerous functional uses, fulfilling roles in the delicatessen, the drugstore, and the supermarket.

above The tumbling purple sage and rosemary seem to want to join the formal mats of thyme that point to the sundial. This very uncomplicated herb garden is in perfect keeping with the aged priory building.

opposite A terracotta forcing jar is a focal point for a mix of herbs and ornamentals including golden marjoram, *Atriplex hortensis* var. *rubra*, rue, *Phacelia campanularia*, bronze fennel, and cotton lavender.

An herb can be any "plant that has a culinary or curative use," which means that several hundred plants are defined as herbs. Herbs were traditionally used in the kitchen as foodstuffs, both fresh and dried, but before the advent of the pharmaceutical industry, they were also the main source of medicines, their names often reflecting their use—examples being woundwort and eyebright. Indeed, there is currently a renaissance of interest in the medicinal qualities of certain herbs. Pharmaceutical companies are scouring old Herbals and the world's jungles in search of plants with curative properties, such

left This sunken garden in Santa Barbara takes full advantage of its unusual topography and uses raised beds to repeat the theme of the walls. To tone down the geometry, the beds are filled with a free-growing display of herbs, and pots of herbs further soften the edges.

opposite Even the most uncomplicated garden layout can be enlivened with a feast of herbs. French lavender and chives poke their flowers into shot, while purple sage, mint, and catmint tumble over the path, and fennel and garden sorrel add their upright stature.

as Saint-John's wort (*Hypericum perforatum*), which is acknowledged as a mild antidepressant. Herb oils are also extracted and distilled into essential oils used in aromatherapy. (You should always take professional advice before you use or take any herbal product for medicinal purposes.)

Herbs were also used widely within the house, where they were both ornamental and utilitarian. Potpourri containing scented leaves and flowers (typically rose petals, lavender, lemon verbena, chamomile, and orris) was used to fragrance a house (a role now shared with herbal oils warmed in a candle burner); and dried herb flowers such as lavender cotton and wormwood were used as decoration. At the practical end of the scale, herbs were used as insect repellents: fleabane kept fleas out of bedding, leaves of the common elder repelled flies, and feverfew deterred moths.

Herbs are intrinsically very attractive plants, and nature has designed them so that the vast majority go together in an aesthetically pleasing manner. In my opinion, while it is possible to make a pig's ear of the garden layout, it is almost impossible to fill the beds with an unattractive display of herbs. This built-in advantage makes herbs a pleasure to work with; they are also great fun, because one can continually experiment with new combinations and arrangements of form, color, height, and texture, safe in the knowledge that the result will vary only in its degree of success. And because herbs are so obliging there are many different ways in which they can be grown for ornament. Traditionally, they were a part of the happy mix that is the cottage garden; but they can be grown in informal drifts, either within a herb bed as part of the productive garden or among an ornamental display. They look equally at home in a formal bed within a formal garden or in a geometrically designed herb bed, but here herbs are the whole garden.

The structure of this cottage herb garden is formal, but uses natural materials throughout. The aim of the hard landscaping is to introduce an attractive, formal structure and shape to the garden, but one that is flexible. The plan shows all the beds planted with herbs, but it would be a simple matter to replace some or all of

them to create a display that is more varied or more traditional. Radiating from the central pool and fountain are sets of overlapping square beds, which are raised to varying heights using thick oak boards, and which contain a tall, square water feature (also made of oak and waterproofed). A central square of weathered brick in basket-weave pattern brings variety to the peripheral surfacing; the flagstone paving is deliberately laid with large gaps between the flags for thyme and chamomile. At the far end of the garden is a semicircular raised bed, which could be used as a seat, but perhaps more comfortable and secluded are the curved benches on the facing side walls. They are also surrounded by raised beds, and positioned so the whole garden can be seen from them.

Herbs fall into three broad categories: shrubby, perennial, and short-lived (annual, biennial, or tender), and this garden makes use of all three. Since I enjoy

beds), and provides a pleasant contrast with the perennial and short-lived herbs, which are planted in informal clumps in the large raised beds.

The ground-level beds nearest the pool are also formally planted, with different types of thyme and basil, which look attractive and scent the air as one brushes past. They are also two of my favorite culinary herbs and are therefore placed within easy reach of the back door for quick harvest. I have extensively used my favorite of all herbs, lavender, both as a backdrop to the curved seating areas, and in bold mass planting as a focal point in the terminal raised bed. I have done so purely for personal pleasure, as I love its leaf color, form, flower color, and scent. However, other herbs would work equally well planted in a mass, or the beds could be given over to a wider range of species. Three types of mint are deliberately grown in pots in order to contain their exuberance (they take over if grown in an open bed), and other pots contain the tender perennial herbs lemon grass and ginger.

Herbs are a gardener's friend: versatile, attractive, and accommodating. Have fun and experiment, either in a purpose-built herb garden, by filling in with them where ever you have the space, or by simply growing them in pots scattered amid the beds.

opposite Herbs are grown predominantly for their foliage, but many have floral attributes. In this composition the silvery foliage of lavender cotton harmonizes with the variegated thyme, and both help settle the hugeness of the cardoon. Its spiky blue flowers also work very well with the lavender cotton's yellow buttons.

left The background of the black shed and its white clematis make the foreground herbs even more vivid. This is another example of "just plant herbs together and it will work," as *Lavandula stoechas* subsp. *pedunculata* rubs shoulders with garden sorrel and lavender cotton, and variegated sage adds variety.

below The reverse view of the Californian herb garden on page 100 shows how a collection of herbs can look great from all angles, and how the structured garden layout and the architectural form of the topiary (here a bay tree) balances the enthusiastic free-spiritedness of the herbs.

cooking, it is planted predominantly with culinary herbs, although many play multiple roles. For example, lavender can be made into an infusion or used to fill pillows; borage flowers are crystallized to make cake decorations and its leaves used to flavour drinks; bergamot flowers enliven salads and potpourri, while bergamot orange leaves flavor Earl Grey tea; and lavender cotton flowers can be dried for decoration and its leaves used in potpourri.

Four specimen shrubby herbs—sage, lemon verbena, rosemary, and Jerusalem sage—are used as focal points in the largest raised beds, and they should be kept tidy with regular pruning. Shrubby herbs that do well as low hedges are grown in the beds nearest the walls, where they are clipped into the same shape as the bed and cut horizontally to the same height as the middle bed. The pruning scheme introduces a formal feel (heightened by four topiary cones of sweet bay in the corners of the

right Herbs are a playful and very forgiving group of plants, and you can have a bit of fun with them. Here the tapestry of the foliage and the flower colors of lavender, basil, nasturtium, thyme, fennel, angelica, and so on is a great foil for the folly behind them.

left Herbs can also be used to set a calm tone, as here where the dark green of the hedge is complemented by the textures and tones of the rosemary and purple sage to generate a peaceful, tranquil. and aromatic setting for the garden seat.

Plants for a herbal garden

1 French lavender (*Lavandula stoechas*)

2 Bay laurel (*Laurus nobilis*)

3 Southernwood (*Artemisia abrotanum*)

4 Purple Sage (*Salvia officinalis* 'Purpurascens')

5 Fennel (*Foeniculum vulgare*)

6 Lovage (*Levisticum officinale*)

7 Chervil (*Anthriscus cerefolium*)

8 Orris (*Iris* 'Florentina')

9 Lemon verbena (*Aloysia triphylla*)

10 Marigold (*Calendula officinalis*)

11 Sorrel (*Rumex acetosa*)

12 Catmint (*Nepeta nervosa*)

13 Chives (*Allium schoenoprasum*)

14 Garden thyme (*Thymus vulgaris*)

15 Wild thyme (*Thymus serpyllum*)

16 Naples basil (*Ocimum basilicum* 'Napolitano')

17 Dill (*Anethum graveolens*)

18 Hyssop (*Hyssopus officinalis*)

19 Cotton lavender (*Santolina chamaecyparissus*)

20 Woodruff (*Asperula odorata*)

21 Purple basil (*Ocimum basilicum* var. *purpurascens*)

22 Cumin (*Cuminum cyminum*)

23 Rosemary (*Rosmarinus officinalis*)

24 Bergamot (*Monarda didyma*)

25 Sweet cicely (*Myrrhis odorata*)

26 Alecost (*Tanacetum balsamita*)

27 Parsley (*Petroselinum crispum*)

28 Thyme (*Thymus serpyllum* 'Snowdrift')

29 Thai basil (*Ocimum basilicum* 'Horapha')

30 Lemon thyme (*Thymus* x *citriodorus*)

31 Lemon grass (*Cymbopogon citriatus*)

32 Ginger (*Zingiber officinale*)

33 Thyme (*Thymus* Coccineus Group)

34 Spearmint (*Mentha spicata*)

35 Peppermint (*Mentha* x *piperita*)

36 Pineapple mint (*Mentha suaveolens* 'Variegata')

37 Coriander (*Coriandrum sativum*)

38 Lemon Balm (*Melissa officinalis*)

39 Sage (*Salvia officinalis*)

40 Borage (*Borago officinalis*)

41 Lavender (*Lavandula angustifolia* 'Alba')

42 Wormwood (*Artemisia absinthium*)

43 Fine-leaved or Greek basil (*Ocimum basilicum* var. *minimum*)

44 Thyme (*Thymus* 'Doone Valley')

45 Garden thyme (*Thymus vulgaris* 'Silver Posie')

46 French Tarragon (*Artemisia dracunculus*)

47 Rue (*Ruta graveolens* 'Jackman's Blue')

48 Caraway (*Carum carvi*)

49 Sweet marjoram (*Origanum majorana*)

50 Jerusalem sage (*Phlomis fruticosa*)

51 Purple fennel (*Foeniculum vulgare* 'Purpureum')

52 Oregano, wild marjoram (*Origanum vulgare*)

53 Feverfew (*Tanacetum parthenium*)

54 Chamomile (*Chamaemelum nobile*)

harvest

The cottage garden has traditionally been a pleasant and harmonious blend of production and ornament. When we think of harvest, our first thoughts are probably of a rich spread of edible crops. But many plants produce material that can be used to decorate the house.

opposite This Swedish garden in Stockholm has that warm end-of-summer glow, the anticipation before the harvest. The prickly globe flowers of the globe thistle (*Echinops ritro*) make excellent additions to a display of dried flowers, as do ornamental grass seed heads, such as those of *Calamagrostis* x *acutiflora* 'Karl Foerster'.

above right *Eryngium* species come in a range of shapes and sizes, but all have this wonderfully spiky architectural form, and in this case a metallic blue coloring. They make a great dried display on their own, or they can be inserted in a living display.

below right The golden colors of harvest—this arrangement of flat-flowering plates of *Achillea* and the dainty hair-like grass *Stipa tenuissima* looks great in the garden, and could be easily continued indoors as a dried arrangement.

It is one of the great delights of a harvest garden that much of the harvesting material. be this sculptural branches and twigs, everlasting flowers to be dried, seed heads that can be used in flower arrangements or alone as internal natural sculpture, or attractive berries or fruits, is produced towards the end of the growing season.

Therefore, if planned properly, the harvest garden can operate as a fully functional ornamental garden for the better part of the gardening year, and then give you a big bonus when most other gardens are beginning to fade away. This is exactly the aim of this harvest cottage garden. The planting is designed to create an aesthetic display that is attractive to look at while the plants are growing; but it really comes into its own towards the end of the growing year when it will yield up a bounty of decorative material, as well as a harvest of herbs, whose foliage and flowers, together with dried rose petals, can be used to fragrance the house in the form of potpourri.

But while the Harvest plan (see page 113) is planted solely with the aim of harvestability, it is possible that after a couple of years I might want a change so, with practicality aforethought, it has been designed to be flexible. The layout and structure of the beds gives the garden an intrinsic interest value of form, shape, and height, which is complemented by the paving and rill. With very little effort the garden can be adapted to fulfil a new role with a completely new mix of planting, be this a mix of harvest and ornamental; herbal and edible; ornamental and edible; or any other permutation of these plants, while still retaining its built-in aesthetic

Adjacent to the house is a practical patio seating area, paved with a mix of regularly shaped limestone flags laid

above There are a number of varieties of masterwort (*Astrantia major*) which come in a range of colors from white through pink to this rich wine red. An attractive idea could be to grow a number of different ones from which to create a dried display.

above right Allowing plants to go to seed is not often done these days; we often take the lazy option and buy seed. But, as well as providing a harvest of decorative material, many seed heads, such as *Nigella damascena*, will also yield next year's crop for free.

right With its football-like head of starry, blue flowers *Allium cristophii* is an architectural addition to any bed, but once the flowers have died, the seed heads are also very decorative, and can be effectively spray-painted different colors.

in a rustic, random pattern. A contrasting slate stepping-stone fords the enclosing rill that runs around the garden's perimeter, its arching fountains introducing movement and sound, and giving the garden a slightly exotic feel. The harvest garden layout is based on the traditional cottage garden quatrefoil principle, but the plan is open and the four quarters are not separated by trellis or espaliered fruit trees. Moreover, the pattern of the traditional square bed has been modified to make it more ornamental, and parts of it have been raised using red brick walls to introduce a vertical dimension.

The planting approach is "aesthetic harvest." To introduce a sense of unity within the garden as a whole, the ground-level border surrounding each of the four quarters is planted with the same plant—*Limonium sinuatum* Forever Series, one of the finest hybrids for producing dried everlasting flowers. It comes in a wide range of colors—red, yellow, white, blue, mauve, and purple. The effect of planting lots of small clumps of different colors all mixed together in a random way introduces a note of informality to contrast with the overall formality of the garden structure.

Within each quarter there are two distinct displays: the larger and higher raised bed, and the four lower diamond-shaped beds. In total there are 16 of these diamonds, and the four groups of four are planted with an eye to color co-ordination. Toward the back of the garden are the hotter red and yellow colors, which draw the eye and contrast with the summer greens of the grasses in the taller beds. These will come into their own in the late summer and fall, when their seed heads develop and they don their late-season foliage. The four beds in the front two quarters are planted with cooler whites and blues, which harmonize with the display of ornamental gourds, which are allowed to romp away in their bed (the foliage and summer flowers adding to the show) and the shrubby herbs, which look wonderful together. Finally, within each quarter a centrally placed shrub rises above the surrounding bonanza to act as a focal point. The planting style also varies, both to introduce variety, and for the sake of practicality. In contrast with the *Limonium*, the perennials, annuals, and smaller ornamental grasses are planted in regular straight

left A harvest garden is as much about enjoying the show while it grows throughout the year as using the bounty it yields up. It is also a place where different planting combinations—like this mingling of *Miscanthus sinensis* 'Morning Light' and *Allium nigrum*—can be tried every so often, for new enjoyment and a new harvest.

rows for ease of harvesting, and to link with the formal structure of the garden, while the larger grasses, ornamental gourds. and shrubby herbs grow naturally, but within the confines of their bed.

The range of harvestable plants is really very large, the diversity of the harvestable pieces so big that you can always have a new and exciting range of interior decorations, and the decorative effects that can be achieved while you wait for the harvest to grow so varied and interesting that often the harvest garden will look as if its aim is only ornamental. However, if this "purist" approach does not appeal to you, you can always slip the occasional harvestable plant or outlandish vegetable into an otherwise normal ornamental display and, as a bonus, use it to ornament the house. Remember also that many shrubs with nice berries such as *Callicarpa*, or *Pyracantha*, *Cotoneaster*, or *Berberis* can also be trained against a wall to maximize space in the beds and to create an attractive wall covering.

And just for completeness' sake, if you want a harvestable garden that is full of edibles, but do not want a Potager like that shown on pages 44–45, you can take the quatrefoil plan shown on the Traditional plan (see pages 28–29) and give over all four quarters to vegetables, with fruit trained on the walls and on wires along the paths. The prescribed wisdom with vegetable gardens is to use the four-bed rotation system. This is the system whereby, to minimize pest and disease problems and to balance out soil-nutrition status, each quarter is dedicated to a particular crop group—solanaceous, root and tuberous; legumes and pods; alliums; and brassicas —and at the end of each growing season, the crops are moved one bed to the left, so at the start of the fifth season you are back where you began. Alternatively, it is also possible to cultivate a cottage garden solely with herbs, and to use the resulting harvest for culinary, domestic, and (taking care and professional advice) medicinal purposes (see pages 98–103).

opposite At first glance this looks like "only" a lovely perennial meadow in its full summer glory. But a wide range of the plants—*Achillea*, *Carex*, *Rudbeckia*, bergamot, and *Echinacea*—can be harvested for cut flowers, dried flowers, even herbal use: it really is as utilitarian as it is gorgeous.

left A sweet pea seed head has its own beauty, in its boat-like form, browny color, and the tiny downy covering.

above The seed head of the ornamental grass golden oats (*Stipa gigantea*) is as delicate as it is elegant as it is ornamental. Much of the harvest garden is about what the plant does when it has reproduced, which means a long season of interest in the garden itself.

left With its stunning electric-blue flowers and silver-gray architectural foliage, the tall cardoon (*Cynara cardunculus*) is one of my favourite garden plants. Or is it a vegetable or the source of an exotic dried flower head? The harvest garden can be so productive!

top The apple of Peru or shoo-fly (*Nicandra physalodes*) repels flies, hence its name. Its calyces look a little like another great harvest plant, Chinese lantern or bladder cherry (*Physalis alkekengi*).

above With a little spider perched happily on it, this carrot seed head is what a harvest is all about—the beauty and enjoyment of growing followed by the fun of the harvest to decorate the house.

Plants for a harvest garden

1 *Limonium sinuatum* Forever Series, mixed
2 *Cortaderia selloana* 'Silver Comet'
3 *Physalis alkekengi*
4 *Stipa calamagrostis*
5 *Xeranthemum annuum*
6 *Briza maxima*
7 *Sedum spectabile* 'Brilliant'
8 *Hordeum jubatum*
9 *Astilbe chinensis* var. *pumila*
10 *Salix babylonica* var. *pekinensis* 'Tortuosa'
11 *Zea mays*
12 *Xerichrysum bracteatum*
13 *Dipsacus fullonum*
14 *Iris foetidissima*
15 *Coix lacryma-jobi*
16 *Alchemilla mollis*
17 *Lagurus ovatus*
18 *Achillea* 'Moonshine'
19 *Corylus avellana* 'Contorta'
20 *Lavandula angustifolia* 'Hidcote'
21 *Echinops ritro*
22 *Rosmarinus officinalis*
23 *Nigella damascena*
24 *Phlomis fruticosa*
25 *Eryngium bourgatii*
26 *Santolina chamaecyparissus*
27 *Allium cristophii*
28 *Rosa rugosa*
29 *Cucurbita pepo*
30 *Anaphalis margaritacea*
31 *Gypsophila paniculata* 'Bristol Fairy'
32 *Astrantia major*
33 *Lunaria annua*
34 *Callicarpa bodinieri* var. *giraldii*

cut flower

It is very easy to create a cottage garden whose primary purpose is as a constant source of cut flowers for the house, yet which looks beautiful all year round and which can be used as more than just a harvest zone.

above When growing for cut flowers in a garden that also has an ornamental role, remember to plant sufficient numbers of the harvest plants to ensure that when blooms are cut, there is still an attractive show in the garden.

right A cut flower garden can be integrated as part of an ornamental garden or be its own entity. Moreover it can be planted formally, as above, or informally as here, where the mixture of yarrow, delphiniums, and campanula is as ornamental as it is cut-able.

If only a few displays are required, then the most practical approach is to give a corner of the garden specifically to flowers for the house. Or consider this requirement when planning the garden's design and incorporate sufficient numbers of cut-flower varieties into the scheme so that a little light harvesting will not harm the show, while still providing adequate flowers for your arrangements.

The production of a ready supply of blooms, however, requires a dedicated cut-flower garden. The plan on pages 120–21 shows such a garden, which can also be used for relaxing and living. Nearest the house is a brick-paved, shaded seating area, sweetly scented by the wisteria which scrambles over the top of the pergola. For a longer season of flowers and scent, the planting can be supplemented by climbing roses, jasmine, and honeysuckle. In warmer climes, other appropriate climbers would include *Stephanotis floribunda*, *Trachelospermum jasminoides*, and *T. asiaticum*. For attractive foliage display, you could grow *Vitis coginetiae* and *Parthenocissus* spp.

The juxtaposed square areas are primarily meant for ornament; their simple layout acts as a foil to the busier cut-flower garden. The pools and fountains introduce the calming sounds and sights of moving water and remain visible from the house, while nighttime uplighting introduces another dimension to the display. The terracotta pots, features in their own right, are home to tender species (requiring frost protection) that produce exotic cut flowers: *Strelitzia reginae* (bird-of-paradise flower) and *Hedychium gardnerianum* (ginger lily), whose butterfly-like flowers, while short-lived, produce a sweet scent. Alternative exotic cut flowers include *Anthurium* spp., *Heliconia* spp., and members of the ginger family.

The trellis separating the two garden areas provides support for that loveliest of all (cool) summer-flowering cutting annuals, *Lathyrus odoratus* (sweet pea). It would be equally appropriate and very attractive to plant segments of the trellis with varieties of one color, but I prefer the harlequin effect of mixing the flower colors together. The trellis also offers glimpses into the cutting garden, but to expand the potential view, windows of any shape could be cut into the trellis.

Plants for a cut flower garden

1 *Strelitzia reginae*
2 *Hedychium gardnerianum*
3 *Wisteria sinensis*
4 *Wisteria sinensis* 'Alba'
5 *Lathyrus odoratus* (mixed)
6 *Rosa* 'Zéphirine Drouhin'
7 *Gypsophila paniculata* 'Bristol Fairy'
8 *Rosa* 'Margaret Merril' (Harkuly)
9 *Gypsophila paniculata* 'Flamingo'
10 *Delphinium* (Belladonna Group) 'Cliveden Beauty'
11 *Dahlia* 'Bishop of Llandaff'
12 *Gladiolus* 'Victor Borge'
13 *Rudbeckia laciniata* 'Hortensia'
14 *Iris sanguinea*
15 *Iris sibirica*
16 *Iris orientalis*
17 *Freesia* (mixed)
18 *Alstroemeria* (mixed)
19 *Dahlia* 'White Moonlight'
20 *Dahlia* 'Hamari Accord'
21 *Dahlia* 'Hamari Gold'
22 *Paeonia lactiflora* 'Sarah Bernhardt'
23 *Paeonia lactiflora* 'Duchesse de Nemours'
24 *Paeonia lactiflora* 'Laura Dessert'
25 *Crocosmia* x *crocosmiiflora* 'Golden Glory'
26 *Crocosmia* 'Lucifer'
27 *Crocosmia* x *crocosmiiflora* 'Emily McKenzie'
28 *Lilium longiflorum*
29 *Lilium regale*
30 *Lilium* 'Star Gazer'
31 *Zantedeschia aethiopica* 'Crowborough'
32 *Zantedeschia elliottiana*
33 *Allium giganteum*
34 *Echinacea purpurea* 'White Swan'
35 *Eremurus robustus*
36 *Helianthus* x *multiflorus*
37 *Rosa* Royal Dane ('Poumidor')
38 *Rosa* 'Indigo'

left Even the smallest corner can be used to grow a few flowers for the house, or if the show is just too beautiful it can be left to be enjoyed outside, as here where the bright orange lily stands out against the dusty-blue love-in-a-mist and violet-blue lavender, and all the foliage forms unite.

above The solid simplicity of the huge banana leaves anchor this show, and provide an uncomplicated backdrop for the showy dahlias, while the silvery-green zigzag of the *Melianthus major* leaves introduce vivacity. Just as in a border, so a successful flower arrangement must obey the rules of good design.

all year round

The way to create a cottage garden that looks attractive all year round is to build a strong infrastructure. Augment this with plants with an interesting year-round form, and supplement the framework with plants to introduce seasonally changing interest and diversity.

opposite An all-year-round garden can either be one that all looks good for twelve months, a difficult but not impossible task, or one where different parts of it come into their own at different times, such as this heather bed on a sunny winter's morn.

above right Spring bulbs are a sure-fire winner at the start of the growing season: they can be grown in pots, as a bedding display, or naturalized as here, with *Crocus tommasinianus*, primrose, and *Iris reticulata* rubbing sholders in a very informal show.

below right Summer offers endless opportunities, for the show can be supplemented with tender exotics or bedding plants. Here a "real geranium" (*G. sanguineum*) is at the foot of a bright pink "false geranium."(*Pelargonium*) in its pot, backed by *Astilbe* and flanked by *Iris* and *Primula pulverulenta*.

It is impossible to have a garden in full, perfect bloom for 12 months a year, but it is possible to design a garden that will provide a display worthy of attention whatever the season. One of the most straightforward ways of introducing interest into a garden is to landform. This can be something as simple as creating an undulating lawn, but in the plan shown on page 127, a more dramatic terracing effect is the aim. This is doubly striking, since terracing usually descends from the house, rather than rising at the far end of the garden, as it does in this case. Set at ground level and within an area of two different styles of paving is a knot garden. To introduce variety and to avoid a large expanse of a single material (which always ends up looking as soulless as a parking lot, irrespective of the material used) flat, rounded water-washed cobbles and York-stone paving are combined. The knot garden itself is based on a 17th-century pattern, taken from one of the earliest published gardening books, which inspired many an aspiring gentlemen to adopt the ways of the cottage gardener.

This pattern is relatively complex, but you can find simpler designs in books on garden history or on the Internet, or you might adapt a Celtic pattern. It is picked

above The approach to the front door of this wooden cottage in Normandy will be welcoming all year round, for it has a structure of hard landscaping—paving, brick edged bed, a sculptural rock, trellis, and wooden porch—supplemented by seasonal perennials and year-round shrubs—Portugal laurel (*Prunus lusitanica*), *Euonymus fortunei* 'Silver Queen', and *Pyracantha* spp.

right Living all-year-round structure in this Devon garden is imparted by the neatly clipped hedge, and the form and attractive foliage of the Japanese maple. This and the wedding-cake tree (*Cornus controversa* 'Variegata') offer fall color, and an architectural skeleton in winter.

out in dwarf box, and the open spaces within the knot are surfaced with three different types of aggregate—crushed red brick, crushed white limestone, and crushed coal—to reduce maintenance and to give year-round structure. Other aggregates work equally well—for example, different shades or sizes of the same aggregate, or glass beads, for a modern look. Fill the gaps with bedding plants for seasonal variety (but with increased workload); or carefully select bulbs for a display that changes with the months. Along with the knot, the "gateposts" of box, where paving materials meet, and the pots containing specimen corkscrew filbert trees and dragon's-claw willows add further living structure.

Surrounding the knot is an edging of crushed red brick and a rill, connected to the largest of the seven pools, which form the focal point at the end of this horizontal level. To introduce an interesting look, the pool is half recessed into the lowest retaining wall, and on the first terrace, reaching out over the pool, is a classical statue of an aquatic god. The height of the fountain and the subsequent water movement it causes make the pool unsuitable for waterlilies, although fish would be happy.

This pool is fed by a twin cascade, one per terrace, each of which contains a mushroom fountain, which could be uplit at night; the sheet of falling water is achieved by having a glass lip extend out over the pool below. The terraces are retained by vertical plant-covered stone walls. To increase the plant range in the garden, the walls could be sloped at 45 degrees (to catch rainfall) and planted with alpines. The planting varies by terrace. The top terrace is crowned by three pairs of shrubs, selected for their architectural form and year-round foliage (although the tree fern may lose its fronds in cold regions). Other all-year-interest shrubs include *Mahonia* spp., *Fatsia japonica, Ilex* spp., *Garrya elliptica, Pittosporum* spp., *Cordyline* spp., and, in warmer climes, *Agave* spp., *Aloe* spp,. and cacti. The specimens and the large glass boulders (for a more natural look, use rock) are set within a ground cover of soft, dark green moss; *Ribes tricolor*, ivy, or *Ajuga reptans* 'Atropurpurea' are alternative groundcover plants to use in locations too dry for moss.

The main feature on the middle terrace is the large Japanese maple, trained to have an umbrella form and to

reach out and tumble over the retaining wall behind the statue. The *Acer* introduces form, attractive foliage shape and color in spring, summer, and fall, and has architectural shape when bare; it is a perfect subject to be spotlit. The groundcover here is crushed brick, echoing the knot, and through this appears a succession of seasonal bulbs. The design shows summer bulbs, but for winter, try *Galanthus, Eranthis, Leucojum*; for spring, *Narcissus, Anemone, Crocus, Tulipa, Fritillaria, Scilla, Trillium, Iris,* or *Hyacinthus*; and for fall, *Amaryllis, Crinum, Crocus, Cyclamen, Colchicum,* or *Leucojum*. To offer a more formal display, instead of a mix, plant a display of a single genus per season.

The theme on the lower terrace is "light and dark." A row of specimen *Phormium* 'Bronze Baby' rises out of a

right A rock garden or stone wall is a very attractive way to deal with a change in level, and its structure can be home to alpines, another whole group of plants that can bring the additional year-round interest of form and flowers. Here the summer show is dominated by the red rock rose (*Helianthemum* cv.).

carpet of silver-blue *Festuca glauca*, which is surrounded by the blackness of *Ophiopogon planiscapus* 'Nigrescens'. The contrasting light surrounding the statue is a dwarf, slow-growing variegated bamboo. Ornamental grasses are especially good value for introducing all-year color to a garden with minimal maintenance; other useful species include *Briza maxima*, *Hakonechloa macra* 'Aureola' and *Carex*. For a taller, architectural backdrop, you cannot beat bamboos such as *Phyllostachys*.

For a more traditional cottage-garden feel, try a mixed planting of architectural shrubs complemented by evergreen groundcover, through which seasonal bulbs and perennials emerge. To maximize the impact of this type of mixed planting, you should do it on a relatively large scale, although it does have the advantage of working in both an informal and a formal setting.

Another effective approach to an all-year-round look is to create a gravel garden, adapting to the plan for a Dry garden (see page 141). This could be approached in an informal way or in a more formal way, with raised beds covered with different aggregates, perhaps. To ornament the scene, place a range of different sized rocks and stone, a water feature or two and a handful of permanent architectural specimens, supplemented by the seasonal planting of perennials and bulbs. This approach has the added advantage of being relatively low in maintenance.

above In warm climes where the seasons do not change markedly, the range of tender plants available to provide all-year form and structure is as large as it is exotic. In this Australian garden, the plain back ground only emphasizes the wonderful forms and colors of the succulent foliage.

left Another Australian garden, this time in Tasmania, combines an interesting and artistic layout with a display of living sculpture topiary and a contrasting foliage display of trees, shrubs, and perennials, including *Stachys byzantina*, *Alchemilla mollis*, and *Euonymus fortunei* 'Silver Queen'.

right This tropical luxuriance, with banana and *Asplenium nidus* among others, is in fact in New Jersey, where the climate does not naturally support such tender species. The plants are brought out for the summer, and show how, with a bit of work, the most unlikely and unusual all-year-round interest can be generated.

Plants for an all year round garden

1 *Parthenocissus tricuspidata*
2 *Trachycarpus fortunei*
3 *Phormium* 'Dazzler'
4 *Dicksonia antarctica*
5 *Acer palmatum* var. *dissectum*
6 *Pyracantha* 'Orange Glow'
7 *Hedera helix* 'Oro di Bogliasco'
8 *Pleioblastus variegatus*
9 *Ophiopogon planiscapus*
   'Nigrescens'
10 *Festuca glauca*
11 *Phormium* 'Bronze Baby'
12 *Salix babylonica*
   var. *pekinensis* 'Tortuosa'
13 *Corylus avellana* 'Contorta'
14 *Buxus sempervirens*
   'Suffruticosa'

Planting scheme A

Allium cristophii
Allium flavum
Alstroemeria ligtu hybrids
   (mixed)
Crocosmia x *crocosmiiflora*
   'Jackanapes'
Freesia (mixed)
Lilium longiflorum
Lilium regale
Nomocharis pardanthina

easy care

My definition of "easy care" is "low maintenance"; it's not a euphemism for "no-maintenance garden." That, my friends, is an oxymoron, unless, of course, you want a garden of asphalt dotted with pots of plastic flowers.

above One of the advantages of designing in a natural way, and with a consideration for wildlife issues, is that the result can be attractive to look at, ecologically advantageous, and require less work to maintain—a win, win, win situation!

My first words of advice for making an easy-care garden are "Get rid of your lawn." Lots of grass is nothing but a time waster that soaks up money. Just make a quick assessment of the hours each week you spend mowing the wretched thing, multiply it by the number of weeks of the growing season, then toss in a generous dose of hours for out-of-mowing-season care such as spiking, aeration, weeding, and scarifying. (If you don't do these things, maybe that's why your lawn is a mess!) And finally, estimate the cost of all the tools and the products—mower, edging shears, spiker, fertilizer, weed killer, moss killer, and so on. You will probably have a staggering total of hours, enough for a vacation, which could be paid for

by the money you have spent on sundries! So take my advice for an easier life and grub it all up.

For the devoted novice gardener, the true path to an easy-care garden is to give much of the space to hard landscaping, and to fill the remaining gaps with plants that take care of themselves, and that suppress weeds by forming a dense coverage. The Formal (see page 65) and Dry (see page 141) designs also qualify as "easy care," and demonstrate, I hope, that the hard landscaping approach works equally well for a formal and an informal style. However, with this design (see page 135) I would like to show that an easy-care garden may be created using the cottage garden ethos of growing a diversity of ornamental plants, although to cut down the workload, edible crops are absent.

The garden layout is very simple: a set of three different-sized circles connected by a brick path of weathered brick laid in a 45-degree herringbone pattern. Within an easy-care garden, all solid materials can make effective paths—setts, slabs, flags, tiles, dyed concrete. But avoid loose ones, which can wander, are nurseries for weeds, and require raking to maintain an attractive appearance. However, loose materials can be used as an effective mulch if placed over a semi-permeable membrane, as in the Dry garden, or as here, in the first and second circles, where crushed slate is used as a maintenance-free ornamental surfacing. In both instances, the slate is laid over a mesh, which covers a sump. This water reservoir produces small jets that "magically" appear through the aggregate, with the water just as magically disappearing again.

The granite boulders provide additional natural ornament, and the larger ones could double as seats. However, any inanimate object, natural or man-made, would work well as a low-maintenance focal point—an architectural piece of driftwood, a statue, a sundial, an upturned tree stump, whatever strikes your fancy. Exchanging the granite boulders for tufa and replacing the adjacent top soil with a mix of equal parts of sterilised top soil, sharp sand, and peat substitute, would create the ideal habitat in which to grow alpines. Some alpine plants are demanding, but many, such as *Rhodohypoxsis, Saxifraga, Androsace, Draba, Cyclamen,*

right One of the most straightforward ways to minimize weeding work is to plant a display that has 100 per cent ground coverage, and thus suppresses the vast majority of weeds. Here in Connecticut the ornamental grass *Leymus arenarius* mingles with *Sedum*, *Verbena bonariensis*, *Canna*, and others.

Three master classes in creating a beautiful but low-maintenance display:

left Beth Chatto's dry garden is filled with plants that pretty much take care of themselves. The display is a wide mix of shrubs, herbs, bulbs, perennials, and grasses (*Phlomis*, *Euphorbia*, *Allium*, *Spiraea*, *Cytisus*, and so on), which all have a distinctly architectural but complementary form.

below Piet Oudolf's garden in Holland relies more heavily upon large groupings of perennials, with dotted grasses and bulbs, arranged together to harmonize and contrast. The result is as striking as it is varied.

Helianthemum, dwarf iris, *Narcissus*, and *Dianthus*, grow with little care required. Here, the alpines could be planted both in the alpine bed and in holes drilled into the tufa boulders. Once they are planted, you should cover the alpine bed with a mulch or top dressing of coarse grit, and water the tufa in dry conditions. But do not place tufa or alpine beds beneath a tree, as alpines do not care to be dripped on, and if possible give them a sunny, south-facing aspect. The third circle is a place for table and chairs. Forget iron furniture, which requires painting; powder-coated aluminum requires little care, but may be a touch too contemporary. Hardwood furniture (manufactured from a sustainable source) is the most in keeping with a cottage feel, even though it will require occasional oiling to maintain its color.

The aim of this garden is maximum beauty with minimal maintenance, and the unfussy hard landscaping is a practical foil to the planting. The desired effect is a

above The perennial meadow at Lady Farm in Somerset, looking stunning in late summer, is the most natural-looking of the three examples and uses smaller, regularly repeated clumps of fewer species, including annuals, to create a distinctive look. *Coreopsis*, *Stipa gigantea*, and mullein create the soft yellow-golden show which contrasts with the red *Kniphofia* and blue *Eryngium*.

perennial meadow accented by carefully positioned shrubs. These shrubs are selected both for their interesting all-year-round form and for the additional seasonal interest they can offer. They are positioned so that most of those with winter and spring interest are nearest to the house, to be enjoyed from indoors when the weather is poor, with the occasional point of interest in the distance. Thus, the evergreen, variegated foliage of *Daphne odora* 'Aureomarginata' is supplemented in early spring by its sweetly smelling flowers; the architectural evergreen form of *Mahonia* x *media* 'Charity' has perfumed, bright yellow flowers in winter; *Viburnum carlesii* has richly scented white-pink flowers in spring and a great display of fall foliage, which counterpoints that of the Japanese maples.

Other good shrubs that provide more than just a pretty year-round form include *Hamamelis* spp., *Corokia cotoneaster*, lavender, *Trachycarpus fortunei*, *Euonymus*, and various forms of *Cornus alba*. For decoration on the walls, there are *Itea ilicifolia*, *Parthenocissus*, ivy (although it can become a tad invasive), and *Clematis* spp. And, of course, you can always supplement the summer display with tender plants in pots—for example *Protea* spp., *Strelitzia reginae*, *Agave* spp., or *Heliconia* spp.

prevailing climate—it is pointless trying to overwinter desert cacti outside in Denver! But this wise rule does not restrict plant selection to only those plants that are indigenous to your area. Certainly the local flora will give the most natural look, but introducing plants from a similar climate elsewhere in the world will result in dramatic displays. In an area of higher rainfall, you can select plants that look desert-like (those with architectural foliage and form), sow annuals from dry climates that will survive the season, and experiment. It is surprising how tolerant of an average level of rainfall many drought-tolerant species are and, conversely, how many normal plants will flourish in low-rainfall areas.

Another great advantage of a dry garden is that it requires very little maintenance. Once established, shrubs and perennials will require only occasional pruning and deadheading, and apart from the job of sowing annual seeds, a bit of routine tidying up and feeding is all that is required. But (as always, there is a "but") to achieve good results, weeds must be suppressed. The straightforward way to achieve this is to grow plants through a mulch of aggregate. Doing this also gives the garden an arid look and helps prevent evaporation of soil moisture. The choice of aggregate—gravel, shingle, crushed stone, shale, crushed slate, and so on—is dependent on the desired look. A local stone will give the most natural look; imitation natural scenes can be forged by importing the appropriate surface; and artistic effects are achievable by mixing types, colors, and sizes of aggregate, or by using different aggregates to help define different areas.

On a practical note, surfaces of loose aggregate are best laid over woven polypropylene or a similar permeable membrane. This allows water to seep into the soil below, but prevents weeds from growing up through it and the aggregate from becoming incorporated into the soil. However, a display of annuals growing through the aggregate will require a thin layer of topsoil on top of the membrane and below the aggregate. The depth of aggregate should be ½–1 in (1–2 cm) where the annuals are to grow, 2–3 in (5–7 cm) elsewhere. To ensure that the new plants establish themselves well, dig some manure into the bed prior to laying the membrane, and water the plants with a soluble fertilizer.

opposite Arid-loving plants can be used very effectively as containerized plants to complement a bed or border of dry-tolerant plants and to add another level to the garden construction; in a location which receives "normal" levels of rainfall; or where the climate does not allow tender species to overwinter outside. Here the clay pots of small cacti raised on slices of tree trunk are dominated in the foreground by *Aeonium arboreum*, a native of the Canary Islands.

top left The attributes of arid plants, and for that matter, many architectural species period, are often best shown off when planted in a bed that is then mulched with a stone aggregate, such as gravel, crushed lava, or cobbles.

centre left There is a beautiful contrast between the delicate, silvery foliage of *Celmisia spedenii* and the rich yellow flowers of *Tropaeolum polyphyllum*. Both are complemented by the groundcover of rounded, gray gravel.

below left A close-up of *Cassula undulata* and *Aloe mitriformis* reveals just how beautiful even the smallest display of arid-loving plants can be; which makes them perfect for an indoor display if you cannot grow them outside.

The plan opposite shows a natural-looking garden with artistic additions, planted with species native to a range of countries. A more formal design, perhaps based on geometric beds and borders, with planting designed around a single native species, would be equally suitable. A "hilly" topography has been created by forming the ground prior to laying the membrane, to increase the level of interest. The aggregates used define the different areas, and their use throughout introduces unity to the overall layout.

Wooden steps from the house give access to the sunken path, surfaced with crushed gray slate. This winds its way through a "valley" to the steps that ascend to the wooden-framed and glass-sided hexagonal summerhouse, which looks out over the whole garden. The raised border adjacent to the path is gently mounded to increase the sunken feel of the path and, like a traditional cottage garden path, is sown with annuals, which also cover the mound's sides. The species mix comprises brightly coloured South African annuals; other natural mixes include alpine, Californian, or Mexican desert mixes or a wildflower mix. To achieve a natural look, the seed is mixed before it is broadcast. The peaks of the raised bed are crowned with a substantial rock, and a pair of proteas further increases the height variation.

The ground-level planting consists of specimens selected for their architectural form, flower colors, and year-round structure. However, where frost is possible, the tender proteas and agaves should be containerised, plunged into the bed during the summer and overwintered under shelter. To maintain the natural feel and to increase the floral interest and diversity, a sub-layer of lower-growing bulbs and perennials, also selected for their architectural form and flowers, has been planted in small clumps, creating a random stippling. Another approach is to plant a groundcover of large patches of different low-growing perennials, through which taller bulbs, perennials, or shrubs could rise. Drifts of different colored and different-sized aggregates, studded with a range of different-sized rocks and boulders and occasional specimen plant would require even less maintenance.

The shapely, weathered rocks introduce another architectural element and double as seats. Looking somewhat unusual, and contrasting with their dry setting, water jets shoot up apparently from nowhere, the water falling back through into the gravel to be collected in a sump. The pumps could either produce continuous jets or be controlled by a computer to produce random spurts. Other forms of ornament could include a beehive oven, or an adobe-style table and bench. Uplighting both water features and specimen plants at night would cast interesting shadows, while candles flickering among the rocks and hills would generate a romantic ambience.

left In a climate where the rainfall is average, then an arid garden also means a low-maintenance one. Select plants that require little watering, plant them in a sea of gravel and, hey presto, you have an instant, beautiful and easy garden.

above If covered with a mulch or in a naturally dry area, an arid garden can appear quite austere, which is a positive attribute. But to show this advantage to the maximum, it must contain plants with a form to visually complement it, such as the foxtail lily (*Eremurus* sp.) and *Crambe cordifolia*.

Plants for a dry garden

1 *Fremontodendron* 'Pacific Sunset'
2 *Onopordum acanthium*
3 *Alcea rosea* (white)
4 *Cynara cardunculus*
5 *Corokia cotoneaster*
6 *Protea cynaroides*
7 *Eremurus stenophyllus*
8 *Romneya coulteri*
9 *Callistemon citrinus* 'Splendens'
10 *Phormium* 'Dazzler'
11 *Agave americana* 'Variegata'

Planting scheme A

Allium cristophii
Allium karataviense
Anemone hupehensis f. *alba*
Anemone tomentosa
Crocosmia 'Lucifer'
Euphorbia griffithii 'Fireglow'
Lilium bulbiferum
Nerine bowdenii var. *wellsii*
Nomocharis pardanthina

Planting scheme B

Diascia cardiosepala
Dorotheanthus bellidiformis
Felicia bergeriana 'Cub Scout'
Felicia elongata
Grielum humifusum
Heliophila coronopifolia
Heliophila longifolia
Nemesia barbata
Nemesia strumosa
   (pink & yellow forms)
Nemesia versicolor
Polycarena cephalophora
Rhodanthe chlorocephala subsp.
   rosea (pink and white forms)
Zaluzianskya affinis

plants
for cottage gardens

The following catalog divides up a miscellany of plants suitable for use in a cottage garden by type or growth pattern, so "Climbers", for example, incorporates shrubs that are often wall trained, and "Bulbs" includes corms. In the "Annuals & Biennials" section, plants can be grown as biennials where they are winter hardy; otherwise they can be sown in spring and grown as annuals. Don't be afraid to experiment and try something a little different—that's one of the greatest joys of gardening.

key

Zones

Zones are based on the average annual minimum temperature for each zone, from 1 to 12. The smaller number indicates the northernmost zone it can survive in and the higher number the southernmost zone the plant will tolerate.

Noxious weeds

* indicates that the plant is considered a noxious weed in some states

Plant size

(in inches unless indicated)

⁝ Height

⋯ Spread

Seasonal display

Sp Spring

Su Summer

Au Autumn

Wi Winter

Light requirements

○ Full Sun

◗ Part Shade

Moisture requirements

○ Well Drained

◗ Moist

● Aquatic (i.e. in the water)

Additional Interest

Comments such as "Form' or "Foliage" indicate special features a plant might have other than its flowers.

plant categories

perennials

Achillea
'Coronation Gold'
5–10 ↕40 ↔ 24 Golden-yellow Su ○ △

Achillea
'Lachsschönheit'
(Salmon Beauty)
3–10 ↕40 ↔ 24 Salmon-pink Su–Au ○ △

Achillea
'Moonshine'
5–10 ↕24 ↔ 20 Bright yellow Su ○ △

Agapanthus
'Bressingham Blue'
Agapanthus
7–11 ↕32 ↔ 18 Blue Su ○ △

Agapanthus
Headbourne hybrids
Agapanthus
7–11 ↕36 ↔ 20 Blue Su ○ △

Agapanthus inapertus
subsp. *intermedius*
Agapanthus
8–11 ↕55 ↔ 24 Blue Su ○ △

Agapanthus
'Lilliput'
Agapanthus
7–11 ↕32 ↔ 20 Blue Su ○ △

Alchemilla mollis
Lady's mantle
4–9 ↕20 ↔ 20 Pale yellow Su ◗ △
Foliage

Alstroemeria
Alstroemeria
7–10 ↕40 ↔ 24 Su ○ △

Alstroemeria ligtu hybrids
Alstroemeria
7–10 ↕36 ↔ 24 Orange/red/pink Su ○ △

Anagallis tenella
Bog pimpernel
6–9 ↕6 ↔ 6 Rose pink Su ○ ◗

Anaphalis margaritacea
Pearl everlasting
4–9 ↕30 ↔ 24 White Su ○ △

Anemone hupehensis
Wind flower
5–9 ↕48 ↔ 18 White Au ◗ ◗

Anemone tomentosa
Wind flower
4–9 ↕40 ↔ 18 Soft pink Su-Au ◗ △

Anthemis tinctoria
'E. C. Buxton'
Dyer's chamomile
5–9 ↕40 ↔ 40 Lemon yellow Su ○ △

Anthyllis vulneraria
Kidney vetch
7–9 ↕20 ↔ 12 Yellow/Cream Su ○ ◗

Artemisia lactiflora
White mugwort
4–9 ↕60 ↔ 20 White Su ○ △

Aruncus dioicus
Goat's beard
3–9 ↕80 ↔ 48 White Su ○ △

Astilbe x *arendsii*
'Venus'
Astilbe
4–8 ↕40 ↔ 40 Pink Su ◗ ◗

Astilbe chinensis
var. *pumila*
Astilbe
4–8 ↕12 ↔ 8 Raspberry red Su ◗ ◗

Astrantia major
Masterwort
4–8 ↕24 ↔ 18 Green-white Su ○ △

Astrantia major
subsp. *involucrata*
Masterwort
4–8 ↕24 ↔ 18 Pinky white Su ○ △
Form & foliage

Astrantia major
'Sunningdale Variegated'
Masterwort
5–8 ↕24 ↔ 15 Deep pink Su ○ △
Form & foliage

Bergenia cordifolia
Elephant's ears
3–9 ↕18 ↔ 24 Light pink Su ○ △
Foliage

Caltha palustris
Marsh marigold
4–9 ↕24 ↔ 18 Bright yellow Sp ○
Water

Campanula latifolia var. *alba*
Bellflower
4–9 ↕48 ↔ 24 White Su ○ △

Campanula latiloba
Giant bellflower
4–9 ↕40 ↔ 18 Blue Su ○ △

Campanula persicifolia
var. *alba*
Peach-leaved bellflower
4–9 ↕40 ↔ 12 White Su ○ △

Campanula trachelium
Nettle-leaved bellflower
4–9 ↕30 ↔ 12 Blue Su ○ △

Canna indica
Canna
9–12 ↕72 ↔ 24 Red Su ○ △

Canna indica
Canna
9–12 ↕72 ↔ 24 Orange Su ○ △

Cardamine pratensis
Cuckoo flower
5–8 ↕24 ↔ 6 Lilac Su ○ ◗

Centaurea maculosa
Spotted knapweed
5–12 ↕24 ↔ 12 Pink Su ○ △

Centaurea nigra
Lesser knapweed
3–8 ↕40 ↔ 20 Purple Su ○ △

Centaurea scabiosa
Greater knapweed
3–8 ↕69 ↔ 24 Purple Su ○ △

Centranthus ruber
Red valerian
6–10 ↕36 ↔ 24 Red-pink Su ○ △

Chelidonium majus
Greater celandine
5–9 ↕36 ↔ 12 Yellow Sp–Su ○ △

Coreopsis lanceolata
Tickseed
4–9 ↕18 ↔ 12 Bright yellow Su ○ △

Crambe maritima
Sea kale
6–9 ↕24 ↔ 24 White Su ○ △

Delphinium
(Belladonna Group) 'Cliveden Beauty'
Delphinium
3–8 ↕48 ↔ 12 Sky blue Su ○ △

Delphinium
'Fenella'
Delphinium
3–8 ↕48 ↔ 12 Sky blue Su ○ △

Delphinium
'Sungleam'
Delphinium
3–8 ⫶80 ↔ 12 White Su ○ △

Dianthus
'Alice'
Pink
4–8 ⫶18 ↔ 12 White/red eye Su ○ △

Dianthus
'Brympton Red'
Pink
4–8 ⫶18 ↔ 12 Crimson Su ○ △

Dianthus caryophyllus
Carnation
4–8 ⫶30 ↔ 12 Pink Su ○ △

Dianthus
'Dad's Favourite'
Pink
4–8 ⫶18 ↔ 12 White Su ○ △

Dianthus
'Emile Paré'
Pink
4–8 ⫶18 ↔ 12 Salmon-pink Su ○ △

Dianthus
'Fenbow Nutmeg Clove'
Carnation
4–8 ⫶24 ↔ 12 Red Su ○ △

Dianthus
'Mrs Sinkins'
Pink
4–8 ⫶18 ↔ 12 White Su ○ △

Dianthus
'Musgrave's Pink'
Pink
4–8 ⫶18 ↔ 12 White/Green Su ○ △

Dictamnus albus
Burning bush
3–10 ⫶40 ↔ 12 White Su ○ △

Dictamnus albus var. *purpureus*
Burning bush
3–10 ⫶40 ↔ 24 Pink Su ○ △

Echinacea purpurea
Cone flower
4–10 ⫶48 ↔ 20 Purple-pink Su ○ △

Echinacea purpurea
'White Swan'
Cone flower
4–10 ⫶48 ↔ 20 White Su ○ △

Echinops ritro
Globe thistle
3–9 ⫶48 ↔ 30 Blue Su ○ △

Eremurus x *isabellinus*
Shelford Hybrids
Foxtail lily
5–9 ⫶60 ↔ 24 Pale yellow Su ○ △

Eremurus x *isabellinus*
Shelford Hybrids
Foxtail lily
5–9 ⫶60 ↔ 24 Yellow Su ○ △

Eremurus x *isabellinus*
Shelford Hybrids
Foxtail lily
5–9 ⫶60 ↔ 24 Pale pink Su ○ △

Eremurus x *isabellinus*
Shelford hybrids
Foxtail lily
5–9 ⫶60 ↔ 24 White Su ○ △

Eremurus robustus
Foxtail lily
6–9 ⫶88 ↔ 40 Pink Su ○ △

Eremurus stenophyllus
Foxtail lily
5–9 ⫶60 ↔ 24 Clear yellow Su ○ △

Eryngium bourgatii
Eryngium
5–10 ⫶24 ↔ 12 Lilac-blue Su ○ △
Form

Eryngium giganteum
Eryngium
6–10 ⫶48 ↔ 30 Blue Su ○ △
Form

Eryngium x *oliverianum*
Eryngium
5–10 ⫶40 ↔ 24 Lavender blue Su ○ △
Form

Eupatorium cannabinum
Hemp agrimony
3–9 ⫶80 ↔ 24 White/Red/Mauve
Su–Au ○ △

Euphorbia griffithii
'Fireglow'
Spurge
4–10 ⫶40 ↔ 24 Orange-red Su ○ ◗
Foliage

Filipendula ulmaria
Meadowsweet
4–10 ⫶12 ↔ 12 White Su ◗ ◗

Fragaria vesca
Wild strawberry
5–9 ⫶14 ↔ 8 White Su ○ △

Galium verum
Lady's bedstraw
2–10 ⫶48 ↔ 24 Yellow Su-Au ○ △

Geranium cinereum
Cranesbill
4–9 ⫶6 ↔ 12 White/Pale pink Sp–Su ○ △

Geranium dalmaticum
Cranesbill
5–9 ⫶4 ↔ 8 Shell pink Su ○ △

Geranium endressii
French cranesbill
4–9 ⫶18 ↔ 24 Rose pink Su ○ △

Geranium farreri
Cranesbill
4–9 ⫶4 ↔ 6 Mauve pink Su ○ △

Geranium ibericum
Caucasian cranesbill
5–9 ⫶24 ↔ 24 Violet blue Su ○ △

Geranium
'Johnson's Blue'
Cranesbill
4–9 ⫶12 ↔ 24 Lavender blue Su ○ △

Geranium procurrens
Cranesbill
5–8 ⫶12 ↔ 24 Rose purple Su ○ △

Geranium psilostemon
Armenian cranesbill
5–9 ⫶48 ↔ 48 Magenta Su ○ △

Geranium pylzowianum
Cranesbill
5–9 ⫶10 ↔ 10 Rose pink Sp–Su ○ △

Geranium renardii
Cranesbill
5–9 ⫶12 ↔ 12 White Sp–Su ○ △

Geranium sanguineum
var. *striatum*
Bloody cranesbill
5–9 ⫶6 ↔ 12 Shell pink Su ○ △

Geum rivale
Water avens
3–9 ⫶24 ↔ 12 Apricot-pink Su ○ ◗

Gypsophila paniculata
'Bristol Fairy'
Baby's breath
4–9 ⫶30 ↔ 40 White Su ○ △
Form

Gypsophila paniculata
'Flamingo'
Baby's breath
4–9 ⫶30 ↔ 40 Pink Su ○ △
Form

Hedychium coronarium
White ginger lily
9–11 ⫶60 ↔ 40 White Su ◗ △

Hedychium gardnerianum
Ginger lily
9–11 ⫶80 ↔ 30 Lemon yellow Su ◗ △

Helianthus x *multiflorus*
5–9 ⫶60 ↔ 24 Yellow Su ○

Hemerocallis
'Blushing Belle'
Daylily
4–9 ⫶28 ↔ 24 Melon-rose Su ○ △

Hemerocallis citrina
Daylily
4–9 ⫶30 ↔ 30 Lemon yellow Su ○ △

Hemerocallis fulva
'Flore Pleno'
Fulvous daylily
4–9 ⫶40 ↔ 30 Tawny orange Su ○ △

Hemerocallis
'Golden Chimes'
Daylily
4–9 ⫶30 ↔ 24 Golden-yellow Su ○ △

Hemerocallis
'Joan Senior'
Daylily
4–9 ⫶24 ↔ 40 White Su ○ △

Hemerocallis
'Luxury Lace'
Daylily
4–9 ⫶30 ↔ 24 Lavender pink Su ○ △

Hemerocallis
'Mauna Loa'
Daylily
4–9 ⫶22 ↔ 40 Tangerine-ornage Su ○ △

Hemerocallis
'Millie Schlumpf'
Daylily
4–9 ⫶20 ↔ 24 Pale pink Su ○ △

Hemerocallis
'Scarlet Orbit'
Daylily
4–9 ⫶20 ↔ 26 Scarlet Su ○ △

Hemerocallis
'Siloam Virginia Henson'
Daylily
4–9 ⫶18 ↔ 26 Rose pink Su ○ △

Hesperis matronalis
Dame's violet
4–9 ⫶30 ↔ 24 Violet Su ○ △

Hesperis matronalis
var. albiflora
Dame's violet
4–9 ⫶30 ↔ 24 White Su ○ △

Hosta (Tardiana Group)
'Halcyon'
Hosta
3–9 ⫶12 ↔ 40 Purple Su ◑ ◗
Foliage

Hypochaeris radicata
Spotted cat's ear
3–11 ⫶26 ↔ 10 Bright yellow Su ○ △

Iris foetidissima
Gladwin
6–10 ⫶40 ↔ indef Yellow Su ○ ◗

Iris orientalis
Oriental iris
4–9 ⫶36 ↔ indef White Sp ○ △

Iris pallida
subsp. *pallida*
Dalmatian iris
4–9 ⫶36 ↔ indef Lilac-blue Sp-Su ○ △

Iris pseudacorus
Yellow flag
5–10 ⫶80 ↔ indef Golden-yellow
Su–Au ◗ ◑

Knautia arvensis
Field scabious
4–9 ⫶48 ↔ 18 Lilac-blue Su ○ △

Knautia macedonica
5–10 ⫶30 ↔ 24 Crimson Su ○ △

Kniphofia galpinii
Red hot poker
6–10 ⫶40 ↔ 24 Orange-yellow Su ○ △
Form

Kniphofia
'Royal Standard'
Red hot poker
5–10 ⫶48 ↔ 24 Yellow/Red Su ○ △
Form

*Lamium galeobdolon
Yellow archangel
4–10 ⫶24 ↔ 8 Yellow Su ○ △

*Leucanthemum vulgare
Ox-eye daisy
3–9 ⫶40 ↔ 6 white Su ○ △

Liatris spicata
Gay feathers
4–9 ⫶24 ↔ 12 Rose-purple Su ○ △

Liatris spicata
'Alba'
Gay feathers
4–9 ⫶24 ↔ 12 White Su ○ △

Lobelia
'Queen Victoria'
4–8 ⫶36 ↔ 12 Red Su ○ ◗

Lotus corniculatus
Bird's foot trefoil
4–10 ⫶16 ↔ 4 Yellow-red Su ○ △

Lupinus
Band of Nobles Series
Lupin
3–9 ⫶60 ↔ 30 Mixed Su ○ △

Lupinus
'My Castle'
Lupin
3–9 ⫶36 ↔ 30 Rose pink Su ○ △

Lupinus polyphyllus
Blue-pod lupin
3–9 ⫶60 ↔ 30 Blue-purple Su ○ △

Lychnis chalcedonica
Jerusalem cross
4–9 ⫶48 ↔ 18 Vermillion Su ○ △

Lychnis coronaria
'Alba'
4–9 ⫶24 ↔ 18 White Su ○ △

Lychnis flos-cuculi
Ragged Robin
5–9 ⫶30 ↔ 6 Pink Su ○ ◗

Lychnis flos-jovis
5–9 ⫶18 ↔ 18 Rose pink Su ○ △

Lycopus europaeus
Gypsywort
5–9 ⫶48 ↔ 8 White Su ○ △

Lysimachia nummularia
Moneywort
4–9 ⫶20 ↔ 2½ Yellow Su ○ ◗

*Lythrum salicaria
Purple loosestrife
4–10 ⫶48 ↔ 12 Pink-purple Su ○ △

Malva moschata
Mallow
4–10 ⫶36 ↔ 24 Rose-pink Su ○ △

Mirabilis jalapa
Four o'clock flower
9–11 ⫶48 ↔ 30 Pink/White Su ○ △

Monarda 'Croftway Pink'
Bergamot
4–9 ⫶40 ↔ 18 Pink Su ○ △

Nepeta sibirica
'Souvenir d'André Chaudron'
Catnip
4–9 ⫶18 ↔ 18 Blue Su ○ △

Nymphaea 'Gonnère'
Waterlily
3–10 ↔ 40 White Su ○ ◆

*Nymphaea odorata
Fragrant waterlily
3–9 ↔ 10ft White Su ○ ◆

Nymphaea odorata
var. rosea
Fragrant waterlily
3–9 ↔ 10ft Deep pink Su ○ ◆

Nymphaea
'Odorata Sulphurea Grandiflora'
Fragrant waterlily
3–10 ↔ 40 Yellow Su ○ ◆

Ophiopogon planiscapus
'Nigrescens'
6–10 ⫶9 ↔ 12 Lilac Su ○ △
Foliage

Osteospermum
'Buttermilk'
9–10 ⫶24 ↔ 12 Pale yellow Su ○ △

Osteospermum 'White Pim'
7–10 ⫶12 ↔ 12 White Su ○ △

Paeonia lactiflora
'Duchesse de Nemours'
Peony
3–9 ⫶28 ↔ 28 White Sp-Su ○ △

Paeonia lactiflora
'Laura Dessert'
Peony
3–9 ⫶30 ↔ 30 Cream Sp-Su ○ △

Paeonia lactiflora
'Sarah Bernhardt'
Peony
3–9 ⵊ40 ↔ 40 Rose pink Sp–Su ○ △

Paeonia officinalis
'Rubra Plena'
Peony
3–9 ⵊ30 ↔ 30 Pink-crimson Sp–Su ○ △

Penstemon 'Stapleford Gem'
Penstemon
8–10 ⵊ24 ↔ 18 Lilac-purple Su–Au ○ △

Phlox paniculata
'Balmoral'
Phlox
4–9 ⵊ48 ↔ 24 Rose-mauve Su ○ △

Phlox paniculata
'Harlequin'
Phlox
4–9 ⵊ48 ↔ 24 Red-purple Su ○ △

Phormium
'Bronze Baby'
New Zealand flax
8–11 ⵊ24 ↔ 24 Reddish Su ○ ◗
Foliage

Phormium
'Dazzler'
New Zealand flax
9–11 ⵊ8ft ↔ 3ft Reddish Su ○ ◗ Foliage

Primula aureata
3–6 ⵊ6 ↔ 8 Cream Sp ◗ △

Primula burmanica
Candelabra primula
5–8 ⵊ24 ↔ 8 Red-purple Su ◗ ◖

Primula prolifera
Candelabra primula
6–8 ⵊ24 ↔ 24 Yellow Su ◗ ◖

Primula pulverulenta
Candelabra primula
6–8 ⵊ36 ↔ 24 Deep red Su ◗ ◖

Primula sikkimensis
5–8 ⵊ36 ↔ 24 Lemon yellow Su ◗ ◗

Primula veris
Cowslip
5–8 ⵊ10 ↔ 10 Yellow Sp ○ △

Primula vialii
5–8 ⵊ24 ↔ 12 Blue-purple Sp ○ △
Foliage

Primula vulgaris
Primrose
5–8 ⵊ8 ↔ 14 Soft yellow Sp ○ △
Foliage

Pulicaria dysenterica
Meadow false fleabane
5–9 ⵊ30 ↔ 6 Yellow Su–Au ○ △

Ranunculus bulbosus
Bulbous buttercup
5–10 ⵊ20 ↔ 20 Yellow Sp ○ ◗

Romneya coulteri
Tree poppy
7–10 ⵊ60 ↔ 60 White Su ○ △
Foliage

Rudbeckia fulgida
var. *speciosa*
Black eyed Susan
4–9 ⵊ40 ↔ 24 Yellow Su–Au ◗ △
Form

Rudbeckia laciniata
'Hortensia'
3–9 ⵊ88 ↔ 36 Yellow Su–Au ◗ △

Ruta graveolens
'Jackman's Blue'
Common rue
4–9 ⵊ36 ↔ 30 Green-yellow Su ○ △

Salvia × *superba*
Salvia
5–10 ⵊ36 ↔ 24 Violet-purple Su–Au ○ △

Sanguisorba officinalis
Great burnet
4–8 ⵊ40 ↔ 20 Black-purple Su–Au ○ △

Scabiosa columbaria
Small scabious
5–9 ⵊ24 ↔ 18 Red-purple Su ○ △

Sedum spectabile
'Brilliant'
Ice plant
4–10 ⵊ18 ↔ 18 Red Au ○ △

Stachys byzantina
Lamb's tongue
4–8 ⵊ15 ↔ 24 Mauve pink Sp ○ △
Foliage

Stachys palustris
Marsh woundwort
3–8 ⵊ40 ↔ 12 Purple Su ○ ◗

Strelitzia reginae
Bird-of-paradise flower
10–12 ⵊ48 ↔ 30 Orange/Blue Sp ◗ △

Succisa pratensis
Devil's bit scabious
5–9 ⵊ40 ↔ 12 Indigo Su–Au ○ ◗

Teucrium scorodonia
Germander
6–10 ⵊ40 ↔ 18 Yellow Su ○ △

Trifolium pratense
Red clover
3–11 ⵊ24 ↔ 5 Red-pink Su ○ △

Verbascum bombyciferum
Mullein
4–8 ⵊ78 ↔ 24 Yellow Su ○ △

Verbena bonariensis
8–11 ⵊ60 ↔ 24 Purple-blue Su ○ △

Veronica spicata
'Romiley Purple'
Spiked speedwell
4–8 ⵊ48 ↔ 24 Purple Su ○ △

Vicia cracca
Tufted vetch
4–10 ⵊ70 ↔ 6 Indigo Su ○ △

Vinca minor
Lesser periwinkle
4–9 ⵊ18 ↔ 60 Bright blue Sp–Au ◗ ◗

Vinca minor f. *alba*
Lesser periwinkle
4–9 ⵊ18 ↔ 60 White Sp–Au ◗ ◗

Viola odorata
Sweet violet
7–10 ⵊ6 ↔ 6 Violet Wi–Sp ○ △

Zantedeschia aethiopica
'Crowborough'
Arum lily
7–11 ⵊ40 ↔ 18 White Su ◗ ◗

Zantedeschia elliottiana
Golden arum lily
9–11 ⵊ40 ↔ 24 Yellow Su ◗ ◖

annuals & biennials

Alcea rosea
Hollyhock
3–10 ⵊ60 ↔ 20 Peachy-pink Su ○ △

Alcea rosea
Hollyhock
3–10 ⵊ60 ↔ 20 Sulphur yellow Su ○ △

Alcea rosea
Hollyhock
3–10 ⵊ60 ↔ 20 Deep red Su ○ △

Alcea rosea
Hollyhock
3–10 ⵊ60 ↔ 60 Pale yellow Su ○ △

Alcea rosea
Hollyhock
3–10 ⵊ60 ↔ 20 White Su ○ △

Anthemis arvensis
Corn chamomile
7–11 ⵊ12 ↔ 8 White Su ○ △

Antirrhinum majus
Snapdragon
8–11 ⵊ36 ↔ 18 Mixed Sp–Au ○ △

Antirrhinum majus
Snapdragon
8–11 ⵊ36 ↔ 18 White Sp–Au ○ △

Antirrhinum majus
Snapdragon
8–11 ⵊ36 ↔ 18 Yellow Sp–Au ○ △

Celosia argentea
Olympia Series
9–11 ⵊ12 ↔ 18 Red Su ○ △

Centaurea cyanus
Cornflower
7–10 ⵊ36 ↔ 12 Blue/Pink/White Su ○ △

Cerinthe major
'Purpurascens'
9–11 ⵊ24 ↔ 24 Purple Su ○ △

Consolida ajacis
Larkspur
7–11 ⵊ12 ↔ 12 Blue/Pink/White Su ○ △

Consolida ajacis
Giant Imperial Series
Giant larkspur
7–11 ⵊ48 ↔ 12 Blue/Pink/White Su ○ △

Cosmos bipinnatus
Cosmos
10–11 ⵊ60 ↔ 18 White/Yellow Su–Au ○ △

Cosmos sulphureus
'Polidor'
Cosmos
10–11 ⵊ16 ↔ 8 Yellow Su–Au ○ △

Dianthus barbatus
Sweet William
4–9 ⵊ12 ↔ 8 Pink/White Sp–Au ○ △

Diascia cardiosepala
9–11 ┆4 ↔ 2 Mauve-pink Su ○ △

Diascia namaquensis
9–11 ┆6 ↔ 16 Salmon pink Su ○ △

Digitalis purpurea
Foxglove
4–9 ┆60 ↔ 24 Purple Sp–Su ◗ △

Digitalis purpurea f. albiflora
Foxglove
4–9 ┆60 ↔ 24 White Sp–Su ◗ △

Dimorphotheca pluvialis
Rain daisy
10–11 ┆12 ↔ 6 White Su ○ △

*Dipsacus fullonum
Common teasel
3–10 ┆72 ↔ 23 Pink-purple Su–Au ○ △
Form

*Dipsacus sativus
Fuller's teasel
3–10 ┆80 ↔ 24 Pale lilac Su–Au ○ △
Form

Dorotheanthus bellidiformis
Livingstone daisy
9–11 ┆80 ↔ 24 Pink-orange Su ○ △

Felicia bergeriana
'Cub Scout'
Blue marguerite
10–11 ┆6 ↔ 12 Blue Su ○ △

Felicia elongata
Blue marguerite
10–11 ┆32 ↔ 12 White Su ○ △

Grielum humifusum
10–11 ┆6 ↔ 12 Bright yellow Su ○ △

Helianthus annuus
Sunflower
4–11 ┆60 ↔ 24 Red Su ○ △

Helianthus annuus
'Eversun'
Sunflower
4–11 ┆60 ↔ 24 Yellow Su ○ △

Heliophila coronopifolia
False blue flax
10–11 ┆16 ↔ 8 Blue Su ○ △

Heliophila longifolia
False blue flax
10–11 ┆16 ↔ 8 Blue Su ○ △

Iberis amara
8–11 ┆12 ↔ 6 White Su ○ △

Limnanthes douglasii
Poached-egg flower
8–11 ┆6 ↔ 4 Yellow/White Su–Au ○ △

Limonium sinuatum
Forever Series, mixed
Sea lavender
9–11 ┆18 ↔ 12 Mixed Su–Au ○ △

Lobularia maritima
Sweet alyssum
7–10 ┆6 ↔ 12 White Su–Au ○ △

Lunaria annua
Honesty
6–10 ┆30 ↔ 12 Purple Su ◗ △

Lupinus mutabilis
subsp. cruckshanksii
'Sunrise'
Lupin
3–9 ┆60 ↔ 30 White/Purple/Blue Su ○ △

Matthiola incana
Cinderella Series, mixed
Stock
8–11 ┆10 ↔ 12 Mixed Su ○ △

Matthiola incana
East Lothian Group, mixed
Stock
8–11 ┆12 ↔ 12 Mixed Su ○ △

Matthiola incana
Brompton Group, mixed
Stock
8–11 ┆18 ↔ 12 Mixed Su ○ △

Matthiola longipetala
subsp. bicornis
Night-scented stock
8–11 ┆12 ↔ 4 Lilac Su ○ △

Myosotis sylvatica
Forget-me-not
5–10 ┆12 ↔ 18 Blue Su ◗ △

Nemesia cheiranthus
9–11 ┆8 ↔ 2½ Yellow/White Su ○ △

Nemesia strumosa
9–11 ┆24 ↔ 3 Pink & yellow Su ○ △

Nemesia versicolor
9–11 ┆20 ↔ 3 Mixed Su ○ △

Nicotiana affinis
Flowering tobacco
8–10 ┆30 ↔ 12 White Su ○ △
Foliage

Nicotiana x sanderae
Domino Series, mixed
Tobacco plant
8–10 ┆12 ↔ 6 Mixed Su ◗ △

Nicotiana sylvestris
Flowering tobacco
8–11 ┆60 ↔ 30 White Su ○ △

Nigella damascena
Love-in-the-mist
6–11 ┆24 ↔ 8 Pale blue Su ○ △

Nigella damascena
Love-in-the-mist
6–11 ┆24 ↔ 8 White Su ○ △

Nigella damascena
'Miss Jekyll'
Love-in-the-mist
6–11 ┆18 ↔ 8 Pale blue Su ○ △

Oenothera biennis
Common evening primrose
4–9 ┆60 ↔ 12 Primrose yellow Su ○ △

*Onopordum acanthium
Cotton thistle
6–10 ┆72 ↔ 36 Pink Su ○ △

Papaver commutatum
Ladybird poppy
8–10 ┆18 ↔ 18 Scarlet/Black Su ○ △

Papaver rhoeas
Field poppy
5–9 ┆24 ↔ 12 Scarlet Su ○ △

Physalis alkekengi
Bladder cherry
5–10 ┆18 ↔ 24 White Su–Au ○ △

Polycarena cephalophora
10–11 ┆10 ↔ 6 Blue-mauve Su ○ △

Rhodanthe chlorocephala
subsp. rosea
Swan river everlasting
9–11 ┆12 ↔ 6 Pink & White Su ○ △
Foliage

Salvia splendens
'Rambo'
Salvia
9–11 ┆18 ↔ 12 Scarlet Su–Au ○ △
Berries & foliage

Salvia splendens
(Vista Series) 'Vista Purple'
Salvia
9–11 ┆12 ↔ 12 Purple Su–Au ○ △

Salvia splendens
(Vista Series) 'Vista Red'
Salvia
9–11 ‖12 ↔ 12 Red Su–Au ○ △

Scabiosa atropurpurea
Sweet scabious
9–11 ‖36 ↔ 12 Crimsom Su–Au ○ △

Senecio cineraria
8–10 ‖12 ↔ 12 Yellow Su ○ △
Foliage

Silene dioica
Red campion
5–8 ‖31 ↔ 18 Pink-red Sp–Su ○ △

Smyrnium Perfoliate alexanders
6–10 ‖30 ↔ 24 Yellow Su ○ △

Tagetes erecta
African Marigold
10–12 ‖30 ↔ 18 Yellow Su–Au ○ △

Verbena iaciniata
'Lavender Mist'
9–11 ‖12 ↔ 12 White, lavender Su–Au ○ △

Xanthophthalmum segetum
Corn Marigold
8–11 ‖18 ↔ 12 Yellow Su ○ △

Xeranthemum annuum
Immortelle
9–11 ‖24 ↔ 18 Purple Su ○ △

Xerichrysum bracteatum
Straw flower
9–11 ‖30 ↔ 12 Yellow Su ○ △
Foliage

Zaluzianskya affinis
10–11 ‖8 ↔ 18 White Su ○ △

Zaluzianskya capensis
Night phlox
10–11 ‖16 ↔ 18 White Su ○ △

Zinnia elegans
'Desert Sun'
Zinnia
10–11 ‖12 ↔ 12 Mixed yellows Su ○ △

ornamental grasses

Briza maxima Greater quaking grass
5–9 ‖20 ↔ 4 Gold Su–Au ○ △
Foliage

Carex elata 'Aurea'
Bowles' golden sedge
5–9 ‖16 ↔ 6 Gold Su–Au ○ ◗
Foliage

Coix lacryma-jobi
Job's tears
9–11 ‖36 ↔ 6 Su–Au ○ △
Foliage

Cortaderia selloana
'Silver Comet'
Pampas grass
9–11 ‖60 ↔ 40 White Su–Au ○ △
Foliage

Festuca glauca
Blue fescue
4–8 ‖4 ↔ 4 Gray-blue Sp–Wi ○ △
Foliage

Hakonechloa macra
'Aureola'
4–9 ‖16 ↔ 24 Yellow-red Su–Au ○ △
Foliage

***Hordeum jubatum**
Foxtail barley
5–8 ‖24 ↔ 12 Golden Su–Au ○ △
Foliage

Lagurus ovatus
Hare's tail grass
9–11 ‖18 ↔ 6 White Su–Au ○ △
Foliage

Leymus arenarius
Lyme grass
4–9 ‖60 ↔ indef Gray-green Su–Au ○ △
Foliage

Miscanthus sinensis
'Gracillimus'
6–10 ‖48 ↔ 18 White Sp–Wi ○ △
Foliage

Phyllostachys aureosulcata f.
aureocaulis
Golden grove bamboo
6–11 ‖25ft ↔ indef Golden Sp–Wi ○ △
Form & foliage

Pleioblastus variegatus
Dwarf white stripe bamboo
5–10 ‖30 ↔ indef White/Green Sp–Wi ○ △
Foliage

Stipa calamagrostis
6–10 ‖40 ↔ 18 Blue-green Su–Au ○ △
Foliage

herbs

Achillea millefolium
Yarrow
3–9 ‖40 ↔ 24 White/Pink Su–Au ○ △

Aloysia triphylla
Lemon balm
8–12 ‖10ft ↔ 10ft Lilac Su ○ △

Anethum graveolens
Dill
8–10 ‖60 ↔ 12 Su ○ △

Anthriscus cerefolium
Chervil
4–9 ‖24 ↔ 12 Su ○ △

Artemisia abrotanum
Lad's love
5–9 ‖30 ↔ 30 Su ○ △

Artemisia absinthium
Wormwood
4–9 ‖40 ↔ 48 Su ○ △

Artemisia dracunculus
French tarragon
5–9 ‖80 ↔ 24 Su ○ △

Borago officinalis
Borage
5–10 ‖24 ↔ 24 Sky blue Su ○ △

Calendula officinalis
Marigold
9–11 ‖28 ↔ 12 Orange Su ○ △

Carum carvi
Caraway
3–10 ‖24 ↔ 6 White Su ○ △

Chamaemelum nobile
Chamomile
6–9 ‖4 ↔ 18 White Su ○ △

Coriandrum sativum
Coriander
6–9 ‖24 ↔ 12 Su ○ △

Cuminum cyminum
Cumin
8–12 ‖12 ↔ 4 White Su ○ △

Cymbopogon citratus
Lemon grass
9–11 ‖80 ↔ 18 Su ○ △

Eruca vesicaria subsp. *sativa*
Garden rocket
7–10 ‖16–40 ↔ 12–24 Su ○ △

Foeniculum vulgare
Fennel
5–10 ‖80 ↔ 18 Su ○ △

Foeniculum vulgare
'Purpureum'
Purple fennel
5–10 ‖80 ↔ 18 Su ○ △

Galium odoratum
Woodruff
3–9 ‖18 ↔ 12 White Sp–Su ○ △

Hyssopus officinalis
Hyssop
6–9 ‖24 ↔ 40 Su ○ △

Iris
'Florentina'
Orris
4–9 ‖32 ↔ indef White Sp–Su ○ ◗

Laurus nobilis
Bay laurel
8–11 ‖30ft ↔ 16ft

Lavandula angustifolia
'Alba'
English lavender
6–11 ‖90 ↔ 120 White Su ○ △

Lavandula angustifolia
'Hidcote'
English lavender
6–11 ‖30 ↔ 30 Blue Su ○ △

Lavandula stoechas
French lavender
8–11 ‖30 ↔ 30 Blue Su ○ △

Levisticum officinale
Lovage
3–10 ‖28 ↔ 8 Yellow Su ○ △

Melissa officinalis
Lemon balm
4–9 ‖60 ↔ 24 Yellow Su ○ △

Mentha x *piperita*
Peppermint
4–8 ‖24 ↔ indef Purple Su ○ △

Mentha spicata
Spearmint
4–9 ‖24 ↔ indef Purple-blue Su ○ △

Mentha suaveolens
'Variegata'
Applemint
5–9 ‖40 ↔ indef White Su ○ △

Monarda didyma
Bergamot
4–9 ⫶40 ↔ 45 Red Su ○ ◖

Myrrhis odorata
Sweet cicely
4–8 ⫶80 ↔ 24 White Su ○ △

Nepeta x *faassenii*
Catnip
4–8 ⫶24 ↔ 24 Lavender blue Su ○ △

Nepeta nervosa
Catnip
5–10 ⫶14 ↔ 12 Pale blue Su ○ △

Ocimum basilicum
Basil
10–12 ⫶18 ↔ 4 Su ○ △

Origanum majorana
Marjoram
7–10 ⫶12 ↔ 12 Su ○ △
Foliage

Origanum vulgare
Oregano
4–8 ⫶18 ↔ 18 Su ○ △
Berries

Petroselinum crispum
Parsley
7–9 ⫶16 ↔ 12 Su ○ △

Phlomis fruticosa
Jerusalem sage
7–10 ⫶48 ↔ 48 Yellow-gold Su ○ △

Rosmarinus officinalis
Rosemary
8–11 ⫶70 ↔ 60 Blue-purple Su ○ △
Berries

Rumex acetosa
Sorrel
3–10 ⫶24 ↔ 24 Su ○ △

Ruta graveolens
Common rue
4–9 ⫶36 ↔ 30 Green-yellow Su ○ △

Salvia officinalis
Sage
6–11 ⫶31 ↔ 24 White Su ○ △

Salvia officinalis
'Purpurascens'
Purple sage
7–11 ⫶31 ↔ 24 White Su ○ △
Foliage

Santolina chamaecyparissus
Cotton lavender
7–10 ⫶30 ↔ 40 Yellow Su ○ △

Tanacetum balsamita
Alecost
6–10 ⫶31 ↔ 12 White Su–Au ○ △

Tanacetum parthenium
Feverfew
5–9 ⫶18 ↔ 18 White Su ○ △

Thymus caespititius
Thyme
4–8 ⫶1 ↔ 8 Lilac-pink Su ○ △

Thymus carnosus
Thyme
8–10 ⫶8 ↔ 8 White Su ○ △

Thymus x *citriodorus*
Lemon thyme
6–9 ⫶4 ↔ 4 Lilac Su ○ △

Thymus
Coccineus Group
Thyme
4–9 ⫶2 ↔ 12 Magenta Su ○ △

Thymus herba-barona
Caraway thyme
7–9 ⫶4 ↔ 8 Lilac Su ○ △

Thymus polytrichus
subsp. *britannicus*
'Doone Valley'
Thyme
5–9 ⫶2 ↔ 12 Mauve Su ○ △

Thymus polytrichus
subsp. *britannicus*
'Snowdrift'
Thyme
5–9 ⫶2 ↔ 12 White Su ○ △

Thymus
'Porlock'
Thyme
5–9 ⫶3 ↔ 8 Pink Su ○ △

Thymus pseudolanuginosus
Thyme
5–9 ⫶2 ↔ 8 Pink-lilac Su ○ △

Thymus serpyllum
Wild thyme
4–9 ⫶10 ↔ 18 Purple Su ○ △

Thymus serpyllum
'Annie Hall'
Thyme
4–9 ⫶10 ↔ 18 Pale mauve Su ○ △

Thymus vulgaris
Garden thyme
5–9 ⫶12 ↔ 12 Mauve Su ○ △

Thymus vulgaris
'Silver Posie'
Garden thyme
6–9 ⫶12 ↔ 12 Mauve Su ○ △

Zingiber officinale
Ginger
9–12 ⫶48 ↔ 24 Pink/White Su ○ △

trees & shrubs

Acer campestre
Field maple
4–8 ⫶36ftm ↔ 25ft Au ○ △
Foliage

Acer palmatum
'Sango-kaku'
Coral bark maple
5–9 ⫶20ft ↔ 20ft Au ○ △
Foliage & bark

Acer palmatum
var. *dissectum*
Dissectum Atropurpureum Group
Japanese maple
5–9 ⫶4ft ↔ 5ft Au ○ △
Foliage

Acer palmatum
var. *dissectum*
Japanese maple
5–9 ⫶4ft ↔ 5ft Au ○ △
Form & foliage

Agave americana
'Variegata'
Century plant
9–12 ⫶6½ft ↔ 10ft White Su ○ △
Form & foliage

Arbutus unedo
Strawberry tree
7–10 ⫶25ft ↔ 28ft White Au–Wi ○ △
Fruit

Betula utilis var. *jacquemontii*
Himalayan silver birch
4–8 ⫶60ft ↔ 30ft Sp–Wi ○ △
Foliage

Buddleja alternifolia
4–8 ⫶13ft ↔ 13ft Lilac Su ○ △

Buddleja davidii
'Black Knight'
Butterfly bush
5–9 ⫶15ft ↔ 15ft Dark purple Su ○ △

Buxus sempervirens
'Suffruticosa'
Dwarf box
6–8 ⫶30 ↔ 30 Sp-Wi ○ △
Foliage

Callicarpa bodinieri
var. *giraldii*
6–8 ⫶8ft ↔ 8ft Au ○ △
Fruit

Callistemon citrinus
'Splendens'
Bottle brush
8–11 ⫶10ft ↔ 8ft Red Su ○ △

Camellia japonica
'Jupiter'
Camellia
7–10 ⫶30ft ↔ 25ft Pink-red Sp ◗ △

Camellia japonica
'Silver Anniversary'
Camellia
7–10 ⫶30ft ↔ 25ft White Sp ◗ △

Camellia × williamsii
'Donation'
Camellia
7–10 ⫶13ft ↔ 8ft Pink Sp ◗ △

Cistus ladanifer
Rock rose
8–11 ⫶4½ft ↔ 5ft White Su ○ △

Corokia cotoneaster
Wire netting bush
9–11 ⫶8ft ↔ 10ft Yellow Sp ○ △
Form

Corylus avellana
'Contorta'
Corkscrew hazel
4–8 ⫶20ft ↔ 20ft Sp-Wi ○ △
Form & foliage

Cotinus coggygria
'Notcutt's Variety'
Smoke tree
4–9 ⫶18ft ↔ 13ft Pink-purple Su ○ △
Foliage

Crataegus monogyna
Hawthorn
4–8 ⫶30ft ↔ 25ft White Sp–Su ○ △

Daphne odora
'Aureomarginata'
Daphne
8–10 ⫶5ft ↔ 5ft White Su ○ △

Dicksonia antarctica
Australian tree fern
8–10 ⫶30ft ↔ 13ft Sp-Wi ◗ ◖
Form & foliage

Euonymus europaeus
Spindle
3–8 ⫶10ft ↔ 8ft Au ○ △
Fruit

Gardenia augusta
Cape jasmine
10–11 ⫶5ft ↔ 5ft White Su ◗ ◖

Heliotropium arborescens
Heliotrope
9–12 ⫶30 ↔ 48 Purple Su ○ △

Hibiscus syriacus
'Diana'
Hibiscus
5–9 ⫶10ft ↔ 8ft White Su–Au ○ △

Iberis sempervirens
7–10 ⫶12 ↔ 24 White Sp–Su ○ △

Ilex aquifolium
Common holly
6–10 ⫶70ft ↔ 20ft White Sp ○ △
Foliage

Isoplexis canariensis
9–11 ⫶48 ↔ 30 Brown-orange Su ◗ △

Lantana montevidensis
Lantana
9–11 ⫶12 ↔ 60 Rose-purple Su ○ △

Myrtus communis
Common myrtle
8–11 ⫶30ft ↔ 30ft White Sp–Su ○ △

Paeonia suffruticosa
'Godaishu'
Moutan
4–9 ⫶7ft ↔ 7ft White Sp–Su ○ △

Protea cynaroides
King protea
8–10 ⫶5ft ↔ 5ft Pink-red Su ○ △

Prunus × subhirtella
'Autumnalis'
Higan cherry
4–9 ⫶25ft ↔ 25ft White Wi ○ △

Quercus robur
English oak
3–8 ⫶80ft ↔ 80ft Su–Au ○ △
Foliage & bark

Rosa × alba
White rose
4–9 ⫶8ft ↔ 5ft White Su ○ △

Rosa
Alec's Red ('Cored')
Rose
5–9 ⫶39 ↔ 2ft Cherry red Su ○ △

Rosa canina
Dog Rose
4–9 ⫶18ft ↔ 18ft Pink Su ○ △

Rosa
'Constance Spry'
Rose
5–9 ⫶6½ft ↔ 5ft Pink Su ○ △
Foliage & bark

Rosa
'Indigo'
Rose
5–9 ⫶6½ft ↔ 5ft Indigo Su ○ △

Rosa gallica
'Versicolor'
Rosa mundi
4–9 ⫶2½ft ↔ 39 Pink/Crimson Su ○ △

Rosa hemisphaerica
Sulphur rose
6–10 ⫶6½ft ↔ 4ft Sulphur yellow Su ○ △

Rosa
Iceberg ('Korbin')
Rose
5–9 ⫶2½ft ↔ 2ft White Su ○ △

Rosa
'Madame Isaac Pereire'
Rose
5–9 ⫶7ft ↔ 6½ft Purple-pink Su ○ △

Rosa
Margaret Merril ('Harkuly')
Rose
5–9 ⫶39 ↔ 2ft White Su ○ △

Rosa
Paul Shirville ('Harqueterwife')
Rose
5–9 ⫶2½ft ↔ 2½ft Salmon-pink Su ○ △

Rosa rubiginosa
Eglantine
4–9 ⫶8ft ↔ 8ft Pink Su ○ △

Rosa rugosa
Hedgehog rose
2–8 ⫶6½ft ↔ 6½ft Purple-red Su ○ △

Rosa
Royal Dane ('Poumidor')
Rose
5–9 ⫶39 ↔ 3ft Orange-red Su ○ △

Salix babylonica
var. *pekinensis*
'Tortuosa'
Dragon's claw willow
5–9 ⫶50ft ↔ 30ft Sp-Wi ○ ◗
Form

Salix triandra
Almond-leaved willow
5–9 ⫶30ft ↔ 20ft Sp–Wi ○ ◗
Form

Taxus baccata
English yew
5–8 ⫶50ft ↔ 30ft Sp–Wi ○ △
Foliage

Trachycarpus fortunei
Chusan palm
6–11 ⫶50ft ↔ 8ft Sp–Wi ○ △
Form

Viburnum carlesii
4–8 ⫶5ft ↔ 5ft White Sp ○ △

Viburnum lantana
Wayfaring tree
4–8 ⫶15ft ↔ 13ft White Sp–Su ○ △

Viburnum opulus
Guelder rose
3–9 ⫶13ft ↔ 13ft White Sp–Su ○ △

Yucca filamentosa
Adam's needle
6–10 ⫶6½ft ↔ 5ft White Su ○ △
Form

Yucca gloriosa
Spanish dagger
7–10 ⫶13ft ↔ 13ft White Su ○ △
Form

Yucca whipplei
Our Lord's candle
8–11 ⫶5ft ↔ 6.5ft White Su ○ △
Form

climbers & wall shrubs

Clematis
Arctic Queen ('Evitwo')
Clematis
5–9 ↕10ft ↔ 3ft Cream Su–Au ○ ◇

Cytisus battandieri
Morrocan broom
7–10 ↕13ft ↔ 13ft Yellow Su ○ ◇

Fremontodendron
'Pacific Sunset'
Flannel flower
8–11 ↕20ft ↔ 20ft Yellow Sp–Au ○ ◇

Hedera helix
'Oro di Bogliasco'
Gold heart ivy
5–9 ↕20ft Sp–Wi ◗ ◇
Foliage

Jasminum officinale
Jasmine
7–10 ↕40ft White Su ○ ◇

Lathyrus latifolius
'White Pearl'
Everlasting pea
5–9 ↕6ft White Su ○ ◇

Lathyrus odoratus
Sweet pea
7–11 ↕6ft ↔ 3ft Mixed Su ○ ◇

Lonicera × *italica*
Honeysuckle
5–9 ↕23ft Yellow Su ○ ◇

Lonicera periclymenum
'Graham Thomas'
Honeysuckle
5–10 ↕23ft White Su ○ ◇

Parthenocissus triscuspidata
Boston ivy
5–9 ↕70ft Au ◗ ◇

Passiflora caerulea
Blue passion flower
4–9 ↕30ft Blue-white Su ○ ◇

Pyracantha
'Orange Glow'
Fire thorn
6–9 ↕15ft ↔ 10ft White Su–Au ○ ◇

Rosa
'Blush Rambler'
Rose
5–9 ↕13ft ↔ 7ft White/Pink Su ○ ◇
Berries

Rosa
'Maigold'
Rose
5–9 ↕8ft ↔ 8ft Bronze-yellow
Sp–Au ○ ◇
Foliage

Rosa moschata
Himalayan musk rose
6–10 ↕12ft ↔ 4ft Cream Su ○ ◇

Rosa
'Zéphirine Drouhin'
Thornless rose
5–9 ↕8ft ↔ 6ft Deep pink Su–Au ○ ◇
Berries

Tropaeolum majus
Nasturtium
10–11 ↕12ft ↔ 4ft Orange Su–Au ○ ◇

Tropaeolum speciosum
Flame creeper
7–10 ↕10ft ↔ 5ft Scarlet Su ○ ◇

Wisteria sinensis
Chinese wisteria
4–9 ↕100ft Blue Su F W

Wisteria sinensis
'Alba'
Chinese wisteria
4–9 ↕100ft White Su ○ ◇

bulbs

Allium cristophii
4–10 ↕16 ↔ 8 Blue Su ○ ◇

Allium flavum
5–9 ↕14 ↔ 3 Yellow Su ○ ◇

Allium giganteum
6–10 ↕72 ↔ 14 Purple Su ○ ◇

Allium karataviense
4–8 ↕8 ↔ 12 Pale purple Sp ○ ◇

Allium schoenoprasum
Chives
3–9 ↕10 ↔ 4 Pale Purple Su ○ ◇
Leaf

Cardiocrinum giganteum
Giant lily
6–9 ↕72 ↔ 36 White Su ◗ ◗

Crocosmia × *crocosmiiflora*
'Emily McKenzie'
Montbretia
5–9 ↕24 ↔ 8 Deep orange Su ○ ◇

Crocosmia × *crocosmiiflora*
'Golden Glory'
Montbretia
5–9 ↕24 ↔ 8 Golden yellow Su ○ ◇

Crocosmia × *crocosmiiflora*
'Jackanapes'
Montbretia
5–9 ↕24 ↔ 8 Yellow-orange Su ○ ◇

Crocosmia
'Lucifer'
Montbretia
5–9 ↕36 ↔ 10 Scarlet Su ○ ◇

Dahlia
'Bishop of Llandaff'
Dahlia
9–10 ↕36 ↔ 18 Dark red Su–Au ○ ◇

Dahlia
'Hamari Accord'
Dahlia
9–10 ↕48 ↔ 24 Pale yellow Su–Au ○ ◇

Dahlia
'Hamari Gold'
Dahlia
9–10 ↕40 ↔ 24 Golden bronze Su–Au ○ ◇

Dahlia
'White Moonlight'
Dahlia
9–10 ↕48 ↔ 24 White Su–Au ○ ◇

Freesia
Supergiant Series, mixed
Freesia
9–11 ↕12 ↔ 4 Mixed Su ○ ◇

Gladiolus
'Peace'
Gladiolus
9–11 ↕66 ↔ 6 Cream Su ○ ◇

Gladiolus
'Victor Borge'
Gladiolus
9–11 ↕66 ↔ 14 Vermillion Su ○ ◇

Lilium
'Bright Star'
Lily
5–9 ↕60 ↔ 6 White/Orange Su ○ ◇

Lilium bulbiferum
Fire lily
5–8 ↕60 ↔ 6 Orange-red Su ○ ◇

Lilium
'Destiny'
Lily
5–9 ↕48 ↔ 6 Yellow Su ○ ◇

Lilium
Golden Splendor Group
Lily
5–9 ↕72 ↔ 6 Golden yellow Su–Au ○ ◇

Lilium lancifolium
Tiger lily
3–8 ↕60 ↔ 6 Pink orange Su–Au ○ ◇

Lilium longiflorum
Easter lily
8–11 ↕40 ↔ 6 White Su ○ ◇

Lilium martagon
Martagon lily
4–8 ↕72 ↔ 6 Pink-purple Su ○ ◇

Lilium monadelphum
Lily
5–8 ↕72 ↔ 6 Yellow Su ○ ◇

Lilium regale
Regal lily
4–9 ↕72 ↔ 6 White/Yellow Su ○ ◇

Lilium
'Star Gazer'
Lily
5–9 ↕36 ↔ 6 White-pink Su ○ ◇

Nerine bowdenii
var. 'wellsii'
Spider lily
8–11 ↕24 ↔ 6 Pink Au ○ ◇

Nomocharis pardanthina
7–9 ↕36 ↔ 6 White Su ◗ ◗

vegetables

Abelmoschus esculentus
Okra
6–10 ⭥48 ↔ 36 Su ○ △

Allium cepa
Green onion
6–10 ⭥24 ↔ 2½ Su ○ △

Asparagus officinalis
Asparagus
3–9 ⭥36 ↔ 18 Su ○ △

Beta vilgaris
Cicla Group
Swiss chard
8–11 ⭥18 ↔ 6 Su ○ △

Brassica oleracea
Capitata Group
Winter cabbage
7–11 ⭥12 ↔ 18 Su ○ △

Brassica oleracea
Gemmifera Group
Brussels sprout
7–11 ⭥60 ↔ 30 Su ○ △

Capsicum annuum
Grossum Group
Sweet pepper
10–11 ⭥30 ↔ 24 Su ○ △

Cucurbita pepo
Ornamental gourd
10–11 ⭥10ft Su ○ △

Cynara cardunculus
Cardoon
7–10 ⭥10ft ↔ 3ft Blue Su ○ △

Daucus carota
Carrot
3–9 ⭥9 ↔ 6 Su ○ △

Lablab purpureus
Lablab bean
9–12 ⭥30ft Purple Su ○ △

Lactuca sativa
Lettuce
6–11 ⭥12 ↔ 12 Su ○ △

Lycopersicon esculentum
Tomato
10–11 ⭥8ft ↔ 3ft Su ○ △

Phaseolus coccineus
Scarlet runner bean
10–11 ⭥10ft ↔ 12 Su ○ △

Phaseolus vulgaris
Snap bean
10–11 ⭥10ft Su ○ △

Pisum sativum
Pea
7–9 ⭥6½ft ↔ 12 Su F W

Raphanus sativus
Radish
6–9 ⭥6 ↔ 4 Su ○ △

Solanum melongena
Eggplant
10–11 ⭥28 ↔ 24 Su ○ △

Solanum tuberosum
Potato
10–11 ⭥24 ↔ 24 Su ○ △

Zea mays
Ornamental maize
10–11 ⭥66 ↔ 18 Su ○ △

fruit

Citrus limon
Lemon
10–11 ⭥30ft ↔ 25ft White Sp ○ △

Ficus carica
Common fig
7–12 ⭥30ft ↔ 30ft Su ○ △

Fragaria vesca
'Semperflorens'
Alpine strawberry
5–9 ⭥4 ↔ 8 White Sp ○ △

Malus prunifolia
'Cheal's Crimson'
Crab apple
4–9 ⭥30ft ↔ 26ft White Sp ○ △

Malus domestica
Apple
4–9 ⭥30ft ↔ 26ft White Sp ○ △

Mespilus germanica
Medlar
4–9 ⭥40ft ↔ 26ft White Sp ○ △

Prunus cerasus
Acid cherry
3–9 ⭥15ft ↔ 20ft White Sp ○ △
Form

Prunus domestica
Plum
5–9 ⭥16ft ↔ 20ft White Sp ○ △
Form

Prunus persica
Peach
5–9 ⭥16ft ↔ 20ft Pink Sp ○ △
Form

Pyrus communis
Pear
4–9 ⭥30ft ↔ 22ft White Sp ○ △
Foliage

Vitis vinifera
Vine
6–10 ⭥30ft Green Su ○ △

acknowledgments

Key:
l = left r = right b = bottom t = top c = center
All images are by Jerry Harpur, except those indicated (MH), which are by Marcus Harpur.

Front endpapers Reading University Botanic garden designed by Richard Bisgrove **p1** Prieuré de Notre Dame d'Orsan, F18170 Maisonnais, France tel: 0033 (0) 2.48.56.27.50 **p2** Claude Monet's garden at Giverny **p3** Eastgrove Cottage Garden, Sankyns Green, Shrawley, nr Worcs **pp4/5** Great Dixter, Northiam, Sussex **p6** Timothy & Christine Easton, Bedfield Hall, Suffolk **pp6/7** Anne Hathaway's Cottage, Shottery, Warwickshire **p8** (MH) East Lambrook Manor, Somerset **p9** Nantucket Island, Massachusetts **p10** (MH) East Lambrook Manor, Somerset **p11** (MH) East Lambrook Manor, Somerset **p12tl** Home Farm, Balscote, Oxon **p12tr** Peter Wooster, Roxbury, Connecticut **p12bl** Timothy & Christine Easton, Bedfield Hall, Suffolk **p12br** Anne Just, Blokhus, Denmark **p14** (MH) Old Rectory, Sudborough, Northants **p15** (MH) East Lambrook Manor, Somerset **pp16/17** Eastgrove Cottage Garden, Sankyns Green, Shrawley, near Worcs **p18** Great Dixter, Northiam, Sussex **p19** Great Dixter, Northiam, Sussex **pp20/21** The Secret Garden (Carol Mercer & Lisa Verderosa), East Hampton, Long Island, New York **p23** Keith Kirsten, Johannesburg, South Africa **p24** White Flower Farm, Lichfield, Connecticut, designed by Fergus Garrett **p25** (MH) Guildford Borough Council garden at RHS Hampton Court Flower Show 2003, designed by Kay Munt & Chris Bruce **p26** (MH) Timothy & Christine Easton, Bedfield Hall, Suffolk **p27t** (MH) Docwra's Manor, Shepreth, Cambs **p27b** Jardin d'Angelique, Manoir de Montmain, near Rouen, France **p30** Ashley & Gilly Meacock, Fudlers Hall, Mashbury, Essex **p31** (MH) Timothy & Christine Easton, Bedfield Hall, Suffolk **pp32/33** Beth Chatto, Elmstead Market, Essex **p34** Eastgrove Cottage Garden, Sankyns Green, Shrawley, near Worcs **p35t** Dr Rivers, Balscote, Oxon **p35b** Frances Denby, Plas-yn-Llan, Llanrhaeadr-ym-Mochnant, North Wales **p38** Patrick & Sylvie Quibel, Jardin Plume, Auzouville, near Rouen, France **p39** a garden in New South Wales, Australia **p40** Egeskov Slotshave, Fyn, Denmark **p41t** (MH) Old Rectory, Sudborough,

Northants, designed by Rosemary Verey & Rupert Golby **p41b** Nancy Fleckler, Oyster Point Gardens, Bainbridge Island, Wa **p42t** (MH) Old Rectory, Sudborough, Northants, designed by Rosemary Verey & Rupert Colby **p42bl** (MH) Francine Raymond, The Kitchen Garden, Troston, Suffolk **p42br** Prieuré de Notre Dame d'Orsan, F18170 Maisonnais, France tel: 0033 (0) 2.48.56.27.50 **p43** Peter Cooper & Karen Hall, Wychwood Nursery, Mole Creek, Tasmania **p44t** Dr Mary Giblin, Essex **p44b** Gunilla Pickard, Great Waltham, Essex **p46** Sir Miles Warren, 'Ohinetahi', near Christchurch, New Zealand **p47** Mme Constance Kargère, Varengeville, Normandy, France **p48t** Richard Hartlage's design for Silas Mountsier, New Jersey **p48c** Keeyla Meadows, Berkeley, California **p48b** Prieuré de Notre Dame d'Orsan, F18170 Maisonnais, France tel: 0033 (0) 2.48.56.27.50 **pp48/49** designed by Jacqueline van der Kloet, Weesp, Netherlands for Mr & Mrs Mol **p50l** Dame Elisabeth Murdoch, Cruden Farm, Victoria, Australia, designed by Edna Walling **p50r** Helen Dillon, Ranelagh, Dublin **p52** Frances Denby, Plas-yn-Llan, Llanrhaeadr-ym-Mochnant, North Wales **pp52/53** Bruno Goris-Poncé, near Grasse, France **p54t** Dennis Schrader & Bill Smith, Mattitock, Long Island, New York **p54b** Great Dixter, Northiam, Sussex **p55** Dennis Schrader & Bill Smith, Mattituck, Long Island, New York **p56** Beth Chatto, Elmstead Market, Essex **p57t&b** 'Dolwen', Llanrhaeadr-ym-Mochnant, North Wales, designed by Frances Denby **p58** (MH) The Laurent-Perrier Garden at RHS Chelsea Flower Show 2003, designed by Tom Stuart-Smith **pp60/61** Piet Oudolf's garden at Hummelo, Netherlands **p61** Mr & Mrs Tim Barbour, Evandale, Tasmania **p62t** Ken & Gwen Davey, Forest Hall, Castlemaine, Victoria, Australia **p62c** designed by Jacqueline van der Kloet, Weesp, Netherlands for Mr &Mrs Mol **p62b** Town design by Jacqueline van der Kloet, Weesp, Netherlands **p63** Wilmar Bouman & Matthew Ryan, Hobart, Tasmania **p64t** Jorn Langberg, Langham, Suffolk **p64b** Cynthia & Chapin Nolen, Santa Barbara, California **p66** Ashley & Gilly Meacock, Fudlers Hall, Mashbury, Essex **p67t** Egeskov Slotshave, Fyn, Denmark **p67b** Timothy & Christine Easton, Bedfield Hall, Suffolk **p68** Charles & Barbara Robinson, Washington, Connecticut **pp68/69** Reading University Botanic Gardens, designed by Richard Bisgrove **p70** Ashley & Gilly Meacock, Fudlers Hall, Mashbury, Essex **p71t** (MH) Eastgrove Cottage Garden, Sankyns Green, Shrawley, near Worcs **p71b** Great Dixter, Northiam, Sussex **p72** a garden in northern France **pp72/73** Great Dixter, Northiam, Sussex **p74**

Eastgrove Cottage Garden, Sankyns Green, Shrawley, near Worcs **pp76/77** Mr & Mrs Harris, Bar Harbour, Maine **p76** (MH) Lladro Garden at RHS Chelsea Flower Show 2003, designed by Fiona Lawrenson & Chris Moss **p78l** Jorn Langberg, Langham, Suffolk **p78r** (MH) designed by Justin Greer, Wimbledon, London **p79** designed by Richard Hartlage for Silas Mountsier, New Jersey **p80t** Linda Cochran, Bainbridge Island, Wa **p80b** (MH) designed by Sarah Lloyd for Askham Bryan College's garden at RHS Hampton Court Flower Show 2003 **pp82/83** (MH) Piet Oudolf's design for Pensthorpe Waterfowl Park, Norfolk **p84t** Ashley & Gilly Meacock, Fudlers Hall, Mashbury, Essex **p84b** Hermannshof, Weinheim, Germany **p85** Ashley & Gilly Meacock, Fudlers Hall, Mashbury, Essex **p86** White Flower Farm, Lichfield, Connecticut, by Fergus Garrett **p87t** Simon Hopkinson's design for Essebourne Manor, Oxon **p87b** Barnsley House, Barnsley, Gloucestershire **p88t** Tim Barbour, Evandale, Tasmania, Australia **p88b** Egeskov Slotshave, Fyn, Denmark **pp90/91** Beth Chatto, Elmstead Market, Essex **p91** Mike Springett, Wethersfield, Essex **p92t** John & Pauline Trengrove, 'Cashel', Ohoka, Christchurch, New Zealand **p92b** Anne Just, Blokhus, Denmark **p93** Beth Chatto, Elmstead Market, Essex **p94** (MH) Piet Oudolf's design for Pensthorpe Waterfowl Park, Norfolk **p95t** Mark Brown, Varengeville, Normandy **p95b** Great Dixter, Northiam, Sussex **p96t** (MH) Timothy & Christine Easton, Bedfield Hall, Suffolk **p96b** Jardin d'Angelique, Manoir de Montmain, near Rouen, France **p98** (MH) Lavenham Priory, Suffolk **pp98/99** Jill Cowley's Garden at Park Farm, Great Waltham, Essex **p100** Cynthia & Chapin Nolen, Santa Barbara, California **p101** Gunilla Pickard, Great Waltham, Essex **p102** (MH) Lavenham Priory, Suffolk **pp102/103** Gunilla Pickard, Great Waltham, Essex **p103** Cynthia & Chapin Nolen, Santa Barbara, California **p104l** (MH) Lavenham Priory, Suffolk **p104r** (MH) The Herb Society Garden at RHS Chelsea Flower Show 2003, designed by Cheryl Waller **p106** Ulf Nordfjell's design for Agneta Sjostedt, Stockolm **p107t&b** (MH) Lady Farm, Somerset **p108l** (MH) East Lambrook Manor, Somerset **p108tr** Villa Ramsdal, Chelmsford, Essex **p108br** (MH) Dr Mary Giblin, Essex **p109** Jaqueline van der Kloet's own garden in Weesp, Netherlands **pp110/111** Green Farm Plants, Surrey, by Piet Oudolf **p111t&b** (MH) Dr Mary Giblin, Essex **p112l &tr** (MH) Dr Mary Giblin, Essex **p112br** Marilyn Grossman, Wisconsin, USA **p114t** (MH) Castle of Mey, Caithness **p114b** Eastgrove Cottage Garden, Sankyns Green, Shrawley, near Worcs **p115**

Frilandsmuseet Open Air Museum, near Copenhagen, Denmark **p116** The Secret Garden (Carol Mercer & Lisa Verderosa), East Hampton, Long Island, New York **pp116/117** Ashley & Gilly Meacock, Fudlers Hall, Mashbury, Essex **p117l** (MH) Castle of Mey, Caithness **p117r** Great Dixter, Northiam, Sussex **pp118/119** Jardins des Paradis, Cordes, France by Eric Ossart & Armand Maurières **p120t** Great Dixter, Northiam, Sussex **p120b** (MH) **p122** Garden House Farm, Drinkstone, Suffolk **p123t** (MH) Mr & Mrs C. Curtis, Haconby, Lincolnshire **p123b** Chiff Chaffs, Chaffeymoor, Dorset **p124t** Constance Kargère, Varengeville, France **pp124/125** Chiff Chaffs, Chaffeymoor, Dorset **p125** Mr & Mrs Royle, Home Farm, Balscote, Oxon **p126t** Jimmie Morrison, Moolap, Victoria, Australia **p126bl** Wilmar Bouman & Matthew Ryan, Hobart, Tasmania **p126br** Richard Hartlage's design for Silas Mountsier, New Jersey **p128** (MH) Gail Adair's garden at RHS Chelsea Flower Show 2003 **p129** White Flower Farm, Lichfield, Connecticut, by Fergus Garrett **p130** Beth Chatto, Elmstead Market, Essex **p131** (MH) Lady Farm, Somerset **pp130/31** Piet Oudolf's nursery, Hummelo, Netherlands **p132** (MH) Beth Chatto, Elmstead Market, Essex **pp132/33** Piet Oudolf's design for Green Farm Plants, Farnham, Surrey **p134** Beth Chatto, Elmstead Market, Essex **p136** Christy ten Eyck's design for Mr & Mrs Binns, Phoenix, Arizona **pp136/37** Mr & Mrs Lerner's garden in Palm Springs, California **p138** Beth Chatto, Elmstead Market, Essex **p139t** Jimmie Morrrison, Moolap, Victoria, Australia **139c** Helen Dillon, Dublin **p139b** Cynthia Nolen, Santa Barbara, California **p140l** Helen Dillon, Dublin **p140** (MH) Docwra's Manor, Shepreth, Cambs **p142/43** (MH) Dr Mary Giblin, Essex **p145t** (MH) Dr Mary Giblin, Essex **p145tc** (MH) Eastgrove Cottage Garden, Sankyns Green, Shrawley, near Worcs **p145bc** Anne Just, Blokhus, Denmark **p145b** Pelham House, Brent Pelham, Herts **p147t** (MH) RHS Hyde Hall, Essex **p147tc** (MH) Dr Mary Giblin, Essex **p147b&bc** Frances Denby, Plas-yn-Llan, Llanrhaeadr-ym-Mochnant, North Wales **p149t** Jacqueline van der Kloet's garden, Weesp, Netherlands **p149tc** Gunilla Pickard, Great Waltham, Essex **p149bc&b** designed by Jacqueline van der Kloet for Ilona van der Enden, Weesp, Netherlands **p151t** (MH) Eastgrove Cottage Garden, Sankyns Green, Shrawley, near Worcs **p151tc** Docwra's Manor, Shepreth, Cambs **p151bc** Mme Constance Kargère, Varengeville **p151b** Peter Cooper, Tasmania **p160** Jacqueline van der Kloet, Weesp, Netherlands **Back endpapers** Wollerton Old Hall, near Market Drayton, Shropshire.

index

Page numbers in *italics*
refer to the illustrations

author's acknowledgments

I should like to extend my deep and sincere thanks to the following, without whom this book could not and would not have made it from idea to printed page. First and foremost, Jacqui Small herself, for her unwavering commitment, wise counsel and faultless judgment in all matters. Also to editorial managers Vicki Vrint and Kate John, to editor Sian Parkhouse, and to Francesca di Stefano, Natalie Villemur, and Eleanor Van Zandt.

Thank you to designer, Maggie Town for another stunning book, and to both Jerry and Marcus Harpur for their magnificent photography and for venturing far beyond the call of duty. And a big thank you to all the skilled and hardworking owners who were so generous in opening the gates of their beautiful gardens to Jerry and Marcus. To illustrators David Ashby (pages 28–9), Sally Pinhey (pages 58-9, 96-7), Lizzie Sanders (pages 36–7, 44–5, 51, 64–5, 74–5, 81, 105, 120-1, 141) and Ann Winterbotham (pages 89, 113, 127, 135), for bringing my designs to life—you perfectly captured in paint what I had in mind. And finally to my agent, Sarah Dalkin, who, as always, has been a star.

At Sterling I must thank Co-editions Manager Michael Beacom, Dorrie Rosen for checking all the plant names, and Chris Vaccari, Director of Publicity.

And because it is now a tradition I must finally thank, for their companionship, Terry the cat, who is joined by Tasso the dog.

Toby Musgrave's web site is at **www.tobymusgrave.com**